Dr. Joan's Mentoring Book

Straight Talk About
Taking Charge
of Your Career

Joan L. Mitchell, PhD,
IBM Fellow
With Nancy Walker Mitchell

Foreword by Telle Whitney
President & CEO,
Anita Borg Institute for Women and Technology

Also by Joan L. Mitchell

Books:
W. B. Pennebaker and J. L. Mitchell, *JPEG: Still Image Data Compression Standard*, Van Nostrand Reinhold: New York © 1993.
J. L. Mitchell, W. B. Pennebaker, C. Fogg, and D. LeGall, *MPEG Video Compression Standard*, Chapman and Hall: New York © 1997.
Books edited:
I. Witten, A. Moffat, and T. Bell, *Managing Gigabytes: Compressing and Indexing Documents and Images*, J. L. Mitchell and W. B. Pennebaker, Editors, Van Nostrand Reinhold: New York © 1994.
B. G. Haskell, A. Puri, and A. Netravali, *Digital Video Compression Standard, An Introduction to MPEG-2*, J. L. Mitchell and W. B. Pennebaker, Editors, Chapman & Hall: New York © 1997.
R. Hoffman, *Data Compression in Digital Systems*, J. L. Mitchell and W. B. Pennebaker, Editors, Chapman and Hall: New York © 1997.
Marina Bosi and Richard E. Goldberg, *Introduction to Digital Audio Coding and Standards*, J. L. Mitchell and W. B. Pennebaker, Editors, Kluwer Academic Publishers: Boston © 2003.

Also by Nancy Walker Mitchell

Nancy Mitchell, *Surviving Your Student Loans*, Booklocker.com, Inc. 2006: Mitchell & Mitchell, LLC: Las Vegas, NV © 2005.
Henderson Writers Group, *Writers Bloc*, "You Gotta do Your Research" a short story, Nancy Mitchell, Mystic Publishers: Henderson, NV © 2006.

Dr. Joan's Mentoring Book

Straight Talk About
Taking Charge
of Your Career

Joan L. Mitchell, PhD,
IBM Fellow
With Nancy Walker Mitchell

Mitchell & Mitchell LLC
Las Vegas, NV

Published by Mitchell & Mitchell, LLC
3315 East Russell Rd, Suite H #216
Las Vegas, NV 89120
www.mitchellmitchell.net

ISBN: 978-0-9795240-0-4

First Edition May 2007

Manufactured in the United States of America

This book is dedicated to Joan's father, William R. Mitchell,
And to Nancy's mother, Jean Hodges,
Early mentors.

Foreword

*F*or any of you who have considered the question, 'What do I need to know to be successful in my career?' this book is an incredibly useful tool. I am pleased to have been asked to write this foreword.

In my current role, I have the pleasure of working with many women who are interested in or engaged in a technical career. There are many pieces of advice that these women receive, but one of the most common is 'find a mentor'. Mentoring has been shown again and again to be the most effective way to empower a career, particularly for women. Although most of my mentors were men—all truly wonderful and helpful—my few opportunities working with female mentors allowed me a very different experience. In particular, those experiences provided the opportunity to discuss a broader range of topics than I was able to cover with my male mentors.

Technical women often find themselves working in environments where there are only a handful of other women, and female Technical Fellows are still very uncommon. The chance for an in-depth series of conversations with a successful technical woman can be a life changing experience. This book allows you to see into the mind and heart of an IBM Fellow, and learn how she made the decisions that led to her success.

My focus may be women, but Dr. Mitchell's focus is people. Almost nothing in her book is targeted to women specifically. Since she mentors and is mentored by both men and women, she knows the special value of each. The information she offers is important to everyone—including her advice to have at least one mentor of the opposite sex.

Dr. Mitchell does not shy away from the many and diverse topics that successful people cope with. As surprising as it sounds, I can't tell you how many times I've answered questions about how to dress. The book's topics range from dress and personal organization, to the more important matter of systematically designing your career Joan's down-home style brings to life the importance of writing skills, the always formidable matter of presentation skills, and the need to be the CEO of your own career. If you read this book, and think about her advice, you can change the course of your career. You are, after all, in the driver's seat.

Thank you, Dr. Joan Mitchell, for this important contribution in area of mentoring, I wish I had had it when I was just beginning my career.

Dr. Telle Whitney
President and CEO
Anita Borg Institute for Women and Technology
March, 2007

Preface

$\mathcal{M}$entors have been important to me all my life. When I was very young, my parents and older sister filled the role. As I grew older, teachers and guidance counselors stepped in. Long before I became an IBM Fellow, I realized the importance of mentors in helping me along the way, both in my personal life and in my career, and I determined to become a mentor to others. Other people helped me and it was only right and proper that I should do the same. Not everyone realizes the importance of mentoring. I certainly didn't in my early years. Of course, a book can't fill the role of a personal mentor, but...

Over the years, I have found many of my mentoring lessons remain the same. A lot of basic information needs to be conveyed before the mentee is ready for more advanced lessons. A book can provide basic information, freeing up the mentor's time for more specific information.

Most of this book is written from the standpoint of an employee rather than an owner or high level executive. It encourages everyone to find mentors and be a mentor to multiple people as a way to improve your work success and work/life balance. Working at IBM for the last thirty-two years has given me wonderful opportunities to impact the world while having fun. I hope this book will help you take your job and turn it into "fun work."

Throughout the book, there is a repeating theme. Do what makes you happy. Follow your passion. Find the style that works best for you. In order to follow your passion, you have to know what your passion is, so be prepared to look inside yourself. Be prepared to examine your work habits, and your personal habits. Until you know yourself, you can't know the right road for you to take.

My own career goal, since 1976, was to become an IBM Fellow. In 2001, I achieved that goal, and I began giving talks—both inside and outside the company —on the importance of mentoring. I spent a week mentoring at the University of Illinois, Champaign-Urbana. During a late-night discussion, some of the students asked for the book they assumed I had written on the subject. That was when the seed to write this book was planted.

Unfortunately, when I sat down to write, I found myself blocked. I couldn't start writing the actual book, even though I had the proposal written and knew the order in which my stories and suggestions should appear. Finally, I hit on the idea of writing e-mails to my father, each of the e-mails telling stories for a specific topic. The dam broke, and ideas flowed.

I've been a story-teller for decades, so most of my advice comes with illustrations from my life. Since the stories come from memory, the quotes and facts should not be taken literally.

This book is aimed at everyone ages from 10 to 90. Young people can enjoy a few funny stories about life in industry. Maybe seeds will be planted to sprout later in their lives. Some students may decide there are interesting problems to solve and fun to be had in corporations, particularly in the STEM (Science, Technology, Engineering, and Math) disciplines. Older folks may reminisce on their life and be encouraged to tell their stories to the next generations. It is the passing on of those stories, which will enable the next generation to avoid the mistakes of the previous. That's not to say the next generation won't make mistakes. Everyone makes mistakes. But if I—or one of my readers—can help someone avoid repeating costly blunders, the book has done its job.

Contents

Part One

The Basics

This book is, in effect, career mentoring by an IBM Fellow. It illustrates how to move up the corporate ladder without stepping on people, and the importance of mentoring to demonstrate leadership at all stages of your career.

Just as the best way to learn something well is to teach it to someone else, the best way to understand how to advance your career is to mentor someone else on how to advance their career. Mentoring teaches the mentor as much as the mentee. My biggest career inhibitor has been ignorance. This book is not so much intended to provide answers, but rather to indicate the questions readers should ask in order to understand their company's culture. As an instructor once told me, "You can choose not to play the game, but you can't choose not to know what game is being played." It is impossible to thrive and grow if you stay unaware of what is happening around you. A mentor is like a co-pilot, helping you to read the map and avoid going the wrong direction on a one-way street.

The Importance of Mentors

Many technically savvy people have not learned all the personal, social, and political skills necessary for the advancements they desire. They remain ignorant of their company's culture, believing working hard and great accomplishments are sure fire recipes for success. They cling to their illusions even when confronted with contrary evidence about reality.

As you move up in the company, more than technical work is required of you. You need to be able to sell your ideas, show initiative, lead a team, have vision, and have impact on more than your immediate team. You need to develop the flexibility to respond with eagerness. A first step toward demonstrating leadership is to become a mentor to multiple associates. Even new hires can mentor others.

This book will help you assess priorities and focus on the 20 percent of your work that has 80 percent of the impact. The phrase, "Work smarter, not harder" shouldn't be translated to mean, "shut up, quit complaining, and get twice the work done because your colleague was downsized out of the company," but rather, "show leadership and grow the part of your job which is growing you. Grow the people around you by mentoring them. This will help the company grow as well."

You can become more promotable by developing those non-technical, interpersonal and leadership skills. These skills include mentoring, communication, personal organization, and social graces.

In today's workplace, leaders are expected to be mentors and to grow the people around them. Future leaders must begin mentoring early in their careers so mentoring is a *well developed* skill before it becomes a *critical* skill. No matter what size the company, employees must understand the importance of continually improving and broadening their skill base. With the exception of Nobel Prize winners, technical expertise is not sufficient for promotions to the highest levels. In order to be promoted, an employee must show initiative. A significant mismatch between an employee's expectations and reality sabotages many promising careers.

Get a Mentor

The solution to my biggest career inhibitor (ignorance) was to seek out mentors. Learning from others is more efficient than making mistakes yourself. Multiple mentors provide sounding boards for a variety of subjects. I select the person most likely to appreciate my dilemma, but I also seek advice from more than one person.

Some advice sessions may be one-shot deals. When I was considering making the switch from Research into Marketing, I asked for an appointment with my vice president. Among other things, he could guarantee me a return ticket to Research when my time in Marketing was up, so I needed to include him in the decision. Three years later, there was a freeze on transfers and his guarantee was the key to my return. I had his promise in writing and it was honored. Can you get the same guarantee? I don't know, but you can't get it without asking. Before you make major career decisions, you need to include your mentors in the decision-making process. They may know something you don't know, and they will definitely have a different perspective on the situation.

Who was Mentor?

When I started thinking about writing a mentoring book, I learned Mentor was a person in Greek mythology. He taught Ulysses' son, so he was a teacher. One way to look at mentoring is to regard it as teaching with a difference. Mentoring does not take place in a formal classroom; it happens all around you, all the time.

Mentoring is the transfer of life experiences, knowledge, and the ways to do things from one person to another in a mutually agreed-upon relationship. Both parties should get something out of the relationship—and it is a relationship. The mentor may be sharing what he has learned, but the mentee has to give back information as well. I find myself pumped up after an effective mentoring session. After all, it is extremely satisfying to hear how someone improved on your suggestions and stretched in the right direction.

Mentoring is not a parent/child, formal teacher/student, superior/inferior or all-giver/all-taker relationship. It is not coerced. This is probably why officially assigned mentors are sometimes less than effective. Neither the mentor nor the mentee chose the relationship, so neither is likely to be heavily invested in its success. Mentoring is not a monologue with one person pontificating and imparting wisdom to another person. Few people learn well in a one-way relationship. There must be give and take.

How do I get a mentor?

Don't be shy. I can still remember being too shy to ask someone to mentor me. I was so grateful when a mentor actually scheduled monthly meetings with me. I started creating an agenda in advance so I wouldn't forget my questions between meetings. I tried to send my agenda several hours in advance of our meeting, so my mentor had frequently found the answers for me before we met.

I recommend the sideways approach to finding a mentor. First, ask a person if they are willing to answer a few questions over lunch or in a brief telephone call. If the informal meeting is successful, I encourage people to take the next step and ask if the person is willing to be a mentor. If I've had several conversations with a person and then their manager calls to ask if I am willing to be that person's official mentor, my answer is almost always, "Yes." I'm more skeptical about entering into the relationship if the person has never talked to me or demonstrated a willingness to learn from my suggestions.

When I mentor for the first time, I share my mentoring rule (developed as an editor). "I'm the editor. I get to make all the suggestions I want. You are the author. It is your book. As long as you convince me that you understood my ideas, you are free to ignore them. After all, it is your life."

Everyone needs at least five mentors

Depending upon a single mentor may be asking too much from one person. One person rarely holds all the information you need. You should seek to learn from multiple people. Mentoring is a voluntary activity, so don't waste energy being disappointed if your first choice doesn't have the time to help you.

I recommend a person find at least five mentors. At least one mentor should already be at the next promotion level. One mentor should be of the opposite sex. Another one should be outside your company. One should be a peer, and one should be a recent hire. "How can a recent hire mentor me?" you ask. How else will you plug into trends on the college campuses? You learn as much from mentoring as you teach.

Asking for honest feedback

The mentoring relationship should not be an exercise in walking on eggs. There must be sufficient trust that honest feedback is possible. How else are you going to learn and grow efficiently? If you don't trust and respect your mentor, you won't trust and respect their advice, so you will be loath to act upon it. Don't always expect to like what you hear. Sometimes we hear things about ourselves that make us uncomfortable. Don't waste time defending yourself. However, if the shoe doesn't fit, don't wear it.
Part of interpreting feedback is being observant of body language. If a mentor is restless and fidgeting, they may not be comfortable telling you the truth, and a sugar-coated version is easy to misinterpret in your favor. If the news is good, why is your mentor uncomfortable? You may need to probe to determine if your mentor's discomfort comes from the information they need to convey, or if there are unrelated reasons for the unease.

Since the news may not always be good, be prepared to deal with criticism gracefully. I recommend you have a standard answer prepared in advance, particularly for unexpected criticism. My usual answer is, "Thank you. I can promise you I will consider what you just said." I don't promise to take it to heart. After I have slept on the advice, I may ask for clarification.

Rejoice when someone wants to tell you what you did wrong. Few people are willing to risk your displeasure to help you grow.

1

Goals

"*If* you don't know where you are going, any road will get you there." Developing goals and being able to articulate your values makes setting priorities easier and leads to quicker decisions. Goals are the first step towards expanding the 20 percent of your work with the most impact (and leading in the direction you want to go) and minimizing the 80 percent of your work with less impact. Goals help your mentors understand what you aspire to achieve. By understanding what makes you happy and finding your passion, you can determine a unique career ladder tailored to you.

It is rarely too late to accomplish your goal. After moving to Colorado, I sometimes went back to New York to work for a few weeks and often stayed with a friend. My friend took me to a graduation party for Clara Miller. Seven years earlier, Clara had decided to fulfill her lifelong dream of earning a college degree. She assembled a five-inch binder of her accomplishments as a professional musician and received significant credits for it. She received her Bachelor of Arts in Music at age 93.

The Importance of Written Goals

After you decide on your goals, write them down. The importance of written goals is illustrated by a story told about the Harvard Business School. A team surveyed past graduates to determine which classes contributed most to their success. They were unable to find any correlation. However, those who claimed to have arrived at school with written goals had made an order of magnitude more money (their criteria for success) 25 years later than those who hadn't clarified their goals in advance. Those who said they graduated with written goals had made three times as much money as those who were still uncommitted. Students are now required to arrive with written goals.

In 1986, I took a two-week Advanced Management class. During the class, we role-played company officer positions. I learned the purpose of mission statements, goals, and plans. One of the consultants claimed all company general managers could articulate their written goals for the organization. Goals allow you to decide what you value before crisis and decision-making time forces you to act. If a decision will satisfy more than one goal at a time, it is easy to approve, since even if an idea or project fails to accomplish one goal, it is still likely to succeed on the other.

At that time, I usually took a long time to decide even unimportant questions, so this appealed to me. As a result of this course, I made a long list of goals, many of them related to keeping up my home properly. Unfortunately, I had no clue how to prioritize. Everything received equal emphasis. My list was finished about the time I put my house on the market eight years later. Prioritizing would have made a difference.

Decide where you want to be twenty years from now, and write it down. Then break down your long-term goal into short-term goals. Make a plan to reach your goal. What must you accomplish in the next ten years in order to be on track to reach that goal? What must you accomplish in the next five years? What should you accomplish this year? What should you be doing today?

Time Management

In October 1988, I learned my transfer into ImagePlus marketing had been approved. I wanted to establish better work habits, so I took a one-day Time Management class. The instructor recommended the book, *How to Get Control of Your Time & Your Life* by Alan Lakein. He had us write down our six-month to one-year, and five to ten-year professional and personal goals. He commented, "If your short-term goals have no connection with your long-term goals, you may have some serious disconnects in your life."

On my professional list was a goal to write a JPEG book. On the personal side, I wanted to visit all of my nieces and nephews and spend quality time with each of them the following year. I spent that time with my nieces and nephews and have continued to do so regularly. Before establishing my goal, I had not realized how easily I could include extended family in my life. This personal goal never interfered with any of my professional goals. The JPEG book was written four years later.

I learned time-management wasn't just about doing things faster; it was deciding never to do some of them. We were encouraged to "just say no." Some tasks can be delegated, particularly if they will grow the delegatee. However, the instructor encouraged us not to pass on make-work projects or unnecessary work. He recommended a file folder or drawer. Requests that don't seem important can be delegated to the drawer. Then, if someone demands the work be done, you know exactly where to find the instructions. If no one follows through, your judgment that it didn't matter was probably right. The folder or drawer is periodically emptied of items more than three months old. With e-mail, I tend to leave such requests in my in-box.

If you decide to create a "later" drawer for things that don't seem important, be prepared to jump fast if your superiors disagree with your judgment. Recently, I tried to see if I could get away without responding to my general manager. It wasn't that I didn't want to answer her, it just seemed impossible to annotate a sixteen-page report in finite time. After the second reminder, I had figured out how to add comments to the necessary sections in blue and then highlight in bold any other relevant information. You are in charge of your career, but your boss is still your boss.

Lakein's book recommends establishing your goals by writing stream of consciousness for a half-hour, as if you are looking back on your life, for six nights in a row. So I wrote, "I am proud that I accomplished ..." I was convinced I had the spiel memorized. On the seventh night, you look over what you wrote and pick out a few of the most important goals. I discovered the early goals reflected what other people expected me to want. The later goals reflected what I actually wanted. I had never recognized how much baggage (and burden) I'd picked up from other people's expectations.

How to write a goal

A goal must be expressed in language that allows it to be measured and completed within a set time-frame. It is useless to write, "I want to be a better person." However, "I want to be a better person by making my bed every day, starting today, and finishing at the end of this year," fits the requirement to be measurable, with explicit start and stop dates. The perennial favorite New Year's resolution, "I want to lose weight and get in shape," is doomed to failure. "I want to lose twenty pounds by cutting out sugar and alcohol in my diet for the next six months," has a much better chance of success. "I want to get in shape by exercising twenty minutes per day, three times per week, for the next year," is measurable and doable. You can always choose to renew a goal, but when you reach the stop date, you will experience a sense of accomplishment. Researchers say it takes about 45 days to establish a new habit.

Once you have decided on a start date, you can make appointments with yourself to work on a particular goal. Some years back, I made that goal to exercise twenty minutes at least three times a week. It has now become a habit.

It is also important to set a date to be finished with the goal and evaluate your success. In the process, you are defining in advance what "done" means. I find it helpful to ask the question, "How much time is this worth?" Sometimes the answer is, "Not enough to even start." If something isn't worth starting, it makes an excellent candidate for the "just say no" category.

Sharing some goals can help you build a support system. Then you are not alone in your long-term endeavors. I vividly remember writing down one goal in 1976, "I want to be the first female IBM Fellow." As part of my plan to accomplish that goal, I went into Marketing for almost three years, from

1989 through 1991, and was determined to write a book in 1992. These things were a part of my plan. Yet I have no memory of communicating my goal to anyone else until 1996. I was afraid people would laugh at my dream. When I asked the person I worked with in Burlington, VT (1995-1996), he confirmed I never mentioned my goal to him.

While on unpaid leave, I realized I had no control over actually becoming a Fellow. But I could insure that my management knew of my goal. After all, they couldn't help me to accomplish something they didn't know I wanted to accomplish. After September 1996—twenty years after I wrote down my goal—every time there was a change in my management, I explained my goal. No one laughed, and no one tried to stop me from achieving my goal.

80/20 rule

You have heard of the 80/20 rule. Eighty percent of your revenue usually comes from 20 percent of your customers. Twenty percent of your customers generate 80 percent of your problems and so on. You can't apply this rule to assign priorities according to impact unless you know which part of your work is having most of the impact. This is a good place to use your mentors. Ask them for their opinion of your impact. I have frequently wondered why it seemed I slaved for months on a project I found exciting to me, but the project never went anywhere within the company. For example, my first patent, ultrasonic printing, never took off.

On the other hand, sometimes just a few days or weeks of my time led to results that were incorporated into products and had definite benefit. Moving the Image View Facility (a mainframe program) to the PC is an example of very little time and effort for huge results. My team's portion of moving the Image View Facility from the mainframe to PCs enabled PC users to view fax documents on their computers and came about as a result of a request from the White House.

Once you have identified where you are having the most impact, make those items priority A. Projects that contribute to 80 percent of the work but only 20 percent of the impact move to your lowest category. Priority Bs will often migrate over time into the A category, but are not an immediate high priority. This includes work being done because a future need has been recognized. As other portions of the research and development come to fruition, your piece may take on a higher priority.

Lakein says any time a little work on your part will help someone else complete their work, you should always assign priority A to the task. I go one step further and say any time someone else's work depends upon the completion of your work, make your work top priority. Back when I was working on the fax standard, the standards person in Boulder agreed to write the proposal. Then one day, he told me, "It is already too late. You will have to wait another year." My instincts said a year later was a year too late. It was critical to have a proposal on the table in Geneva in six weeks.

My manager's manager explained, "Joan, in this company, it's not okay to complain that someone else isn't doing their job because it just became your job." Two weeks later the document was written, but some of the CCITT (International Telegraph and Telephone Consultative Committee) images we received were corrupted. I had to begin the internal clearance process with incomplete tables.

That was when I realized why the regular standards person had been convinced it was too late. More than 50 'clearance' signatures were required and about half the individuals were in Europe. Fortunately, my third level manager became involved and made some phone calls.

The time management instructor also emphasized that any time a little work on your part will enable others to get started, you obviously need to make it a priority A. This view of the world has helped me avoid those last minute crises when it is too late to delegate a task to someone else. What seems like a pesky task to you may be critical to them.

Always make financial items high priority

I can still remember the instructor describing what happens if you don't pay attention to financial tasks and give them high priorities. The financial penalties are painful. He recommended deciding on a safe place (a folder, a drawer, a cubbyhole in your desk) where all bills are stored. Keep stamps and envelopes in the same safe place. Once a week, pay all your bills. This way, nothing is forgotten or lost.

Find your passion

Finding your passion may be harder than you expect. I urge people to use lifestyle choices as one way to zero in on what's important. Even in high school, most students already know if they want an indoor or an outdoor job. Are you someone who wants regular hours or a flexible schedule? Are you bright in the morning, or a night owl? Do you want responsibility instead of letting someone else make the big decisions? Do you want to think about your job after hours, or do you want to leave the job at work? Do you enjoy defining the problem, or do you want the problem to be well specified for you? By the way, you change over time and it is a natural progression to learn to accept more responsibility. Failing to grow leaves you stuck in a time warp.

As a young girl, I dreamed of dancing on my toes. My mother gave me a choice, I could start ballet as a third-grader from the student of my sister's teacher, or I could wait another year and take ballet from my sister's teacher. I couldn't wait. In seventh grade, I transferred to my sister's teacher and spent the next two years relearning everything because I had been using the wrong muscles. Finally, after six years, the teacher allowed me to buy toe shoes. Mom urged me to practice thirty minutes a day if I wanted to perform. I didn't practice. I wanted the end result, but was unwilling to work for it. The experience taught me a valuable lesson. Wishing and dreaming don't get you on your toes. You have to work for it.

Hopefully, you can save yourself six years (or more) by determining early on whether your dream is a hope or a passion. If you have a passion, make a plan and work toward it.

Learn what makes you happy. I learned the hard way when I became isolated in the lab that I need to see and interact with people regularly. Almost everything of significance I've accomplished has been while working as part of a team. I get bored when there is no one to bounce ideas around with, and unless someone else cares, I tend to lose interest. If your excitement and joy in a project comes from interaction, make sure interaction is a part of your working life. On the other hand, if you work best when people leave you alone to do your job, a team environment may not be your best choice.

My work needs to be fun. I'm not talking about easy or light-hearted "fun." For me, "fun" means it is meaningful, it matters to someone else, it is challenging, and it makes a real difference. If my work doesn't matter, I'm not happy doing it. You won't always have the option of selecting your projects, so you need to learn to see the challenge in even mundane things. If your assignment is to make widgets, learn to create the best widgets in the world, and then study those widgets to see if you can improve them further.

It is important to set realistic goals achievable by you. Goals couldn't make me a ballerina. I have the wrong body type, and my passion wasn't there. Part of playing to your strengths is recognizing where they are and learning to compensate for your weaknesses. For example, I don't learn well from hearing. Until I learned to write letters mentally in front of my eyes so I could read back a finished word, I couldn't remember all the letters long enough to identify a word spelled orally. Observe yourself so that you know where your strengths are, then use your strengths to compensate for your weaknesses.

As you figure out what makes you happy, you can write your goals as lifestyle choices. In some ways, lifestyle choices convert professional goals into financial goals. Your goals should include a reasonable estimate of the money you will need to maintain your chosen lifestyle. If you decide you will spend X thousand to live, you look in the tax tables to figure out how much you need to earn in order to clear X after taxes. Don't forget to factor in another 10 percent for savings after taxes. Once you've arrived at a salary goal, you can figure out whether or not your chosen career will support that goal. If your lifestyle goal includes a million dollar house and a fancy car, you probably won't be happy as an elementary school teacher.

Goals are changeable

Goals are not federal laws. You made them; you can change them. However, change them consciously and for good reasons, not by drifting along without thinking. If you are disappointed with your results, maybe it is time to set shorter-term, less aggressive goals. When you are in the habit of succeeding, you can re-examine your original long-term goals and see if they still accurately reflect your passion.

For most of my life, starting in high school, I have tutored others. I assumed I would become a teacher. In high school, my algebra teacher made a big impression on me, so I decided to teach high school math. Then I got to college, and teaching in Junior College looked good. Finally, my first year in graduate school I became a teaching assistant (TA) teaching physics for non-math and non-physics majors (primarily pre-meds).

Professor David Lazarus taught a kind of "physics for poets" class. During a one-hour lecture, he gave eighty demonstrations of the concepts. He shared with me that a good teacher puts in eight hours of preparation for one hour of class. His lecture on waves was so vivid, I was able to invent based on it my second day at the Research Lab.

As a Teaching Assistant, I discovered I didn't like parroting the books. Unfortunately, I had neither experiences nor stories to help the students understand the material. And, I had no patience for the same question, time after time. On the other hand, I still enjoyed tutoring. In the graduate dorm, I often had a chance to tutor. With just a few hours of help, a student would be back in control. The challenge of ferreting out the missing background kept each case different and fun.

While working in New York, I went into Marketing for almost three years. My job was to work on the JPEG standard and to do image education. My goal was to help the marketing and sales folks to "Know what they did know, know what they didn't know, and understand the answers if they asked questions."

In 1996, I taught a semester at the University of Illinois in the Electrical and Computer Engineering Department. The class was an "Introduction to International Data Compression

Standards." On the first day, I warned my students I wanted to give them a taste of industrial life. In the real world, you define the problem, find a solution, and market it—and the only grade you get is staying in business or going bankrupt.

I had a dream. My dream was to teach. Over the years, my dream changed from teaching high school to teaching junior college to teaching at the university level. In the end, I have only taught at the university level a few times. Some dreams take longer to achieve than others. And sometimes a dream is supplanted by a passion. You grow, and goals change. Be prepared to change with them.

"If only" and "Next time"

I once read an article on the two worst words in the English language. To my surprise those words were "if only." Regrets about the past can eat up the future. It is a waste of your time, energy, and thoughts to dwell on the past by creating scenarios based on "if only" I'd done it this way instead of that way. It's okay to say, "I'm sorry, how can I fix it?" It is important to forgive and move on. It is most important to forgive yourself and, once you have learned your lesson from the past, let it go.

Fortunately, the article also offered the two best words in the English language, "next time." "Next time" enables you to learn from mistakes. It is a constructive use of your time, energy, and thoughts to find a better way to handle a situation the next time it occurs. Taking risks means sometimes failing. Letting your failures color the rest of your life gives them a power they don't deserve. I learned in Sunday school that mistakes in mathematics have only the power we give them. As long as we believe the "error," we get wrong answers. As soon as we learn the "truth" (the correct principle for the mathematics), and apply it correctly, we are guaranteed a correct result. Past wrong answers have no power to keep us locked into more wrong answers. This means watching what we think. How we think about things determines whether we continue to grow and learn or remain stuck in regrets.

Never Hold Your Breath

"Never hold your breath" is the advice given to every beginning scuba diver. You can kill yourself if you fail to breathe regularly while under water. For the last few years, I've been involved in litigation over a patent. Thank goodness, I know you can't postpone happiness until the lawsuit is over. You do what you have to do to find the material the lawyers need, and you don't expect to hear from them for months at a time.

Holding your breath is a recipe for accelerated burnout, particularly if you put your life on hold until the big event (for example, your product is ready to ship) occurs. Instead, you should enjoy the 'now'. All you really have in life is a series of 'nows'. Thinking you must wait until after the anticipated event practically guarantees the event will be anti-climactic. There is always another deadline. One product group I wanted to work with continually told me they would get back to me as soon as their current crisis was over. After ten years of waiting, I realized they would always have a current crisis. We never worked together.

Work your goals, but don't hand an event or date in the future the power to determine your happiness. Someone once said, "The journey is the goal, not the end." How we live each day matters more than the conclusion. When you catch yourself thinking, "I'll be so happy when this is over," take a deep breath, and let it out again. Then enjoy the journey.

Pick a date when you will worry

Once you are embarked on a long-term personal or professional goal, don't waste time wondering if you are doing the right thing. In graduate school, many of my friends wasted a great deal of time wondering whether they should be pursuing a higher degree. They had not done the soul searching necessary to find and confirm their passion. This was during the Vietnam War, and the alternative was the draft, so they may have been right to wonder. They may have been attending graduate school for the wrong reasons, but fretting about it didn't help.

Instead of worrying, decide when would be an appropriate moment to reconsider your decision. For example, when I started my Master's I knew applications would be due soon after January if I wanted to change schools or fields for my PhD. I calculated that sometime around December, fifteen months later, would be time enough to initiate a different direction. Until then, I would think and act as if I was committed to the current program and put all my energy into mastering the material.

Once you have picked a date, write it on your yearly calendar. I write it in my Daytimer under the appropriate month for the following year. Later, when I get the monthly calendar for the following year, I transfer the notation, and finally I note it as a reminder on the appropriate day. Now there is no way I will forget. Don't think about changing direction until the notation pops up again. Refuse to doubt or question your decision until the time arrives when you have agreed to reconsider your decision. No worrying allowed.

Decide what "done" means

It is important to document, in your goal or description of a project, exactly what "done" is. Do it before you start, so when you get there you know you're done. I have a cousin who always wrote his high school papers immediately. He started the day he received the assignment. His first step was to decide what done meant. If he decided the assignment should be a three page paper, a three-page paper was what he completed a few days later. He did not allow work to expand to fill the time available.

My third-level manager took me to lunch one day and tried to tell me to decide what was 'good enough'. I had been working several years and should have understood. Instead, I was unreceptive. He used as an example the evaluation of an invention disclosure. He said you can tell quickly if a disclosure is top notch and worthy of a high evaluation. You can also tell if it's bad and deserves to be canned. In both cases, spending extra effort is a waste of company time. He wanted me to save the several-hour process for borderline decisions. His lecture paid off a decade later during the time-management class. I finally understood that always working with maximum effort was failing to use good judgment.

Don't allow the work to expand. Decide what the job entails, and do that. There will be another project, and you want to be free to participate in it.

Handling Setbacks

My first advice when handling setbacks is, "Don't whine about it." Whining is trying to pass the monkey to someone else. As a kid, you could whine to your parents and have some hope they would help you get what you wanted. Of course, my mom couldn't tolerate whining. It was an excellent reason for her to say, "Go to your room until you are ready to stop whining." Your mother doesn't work here—wherever here is. Whining will not get you what you want.

A subtle form of whining is 'blamer thinking'. Blamer thinking occurs in your mind, so others probably don't know about it. Blamer thinking blames others for your problems. "It's X's fault that I can't do what I want." "If only my manager would appreciate my worth, then I could accomplish my goals, etc." Blamer thinking removes the responsibility for solving the problem from you by handing it (mentally) to some one else. It leaves you helpless and disempowered. One reason I'm working hard to get rid of it, is that blamer thinking rarely bothers with reality. It is often pure fantasy and drama with the 'blamer' as the main character.

The biggest problem with whining or blamer thinking is that it encourages a victim mentality. It paints a picture with you in the role of victim and therefore helpless to solve the problem. It prevents you from growing and learning to gain control again. It is a mental process. It happens in your own thoughts.

You can choose what you think about an obstacle. Instead of feeling victimized, you can accept the challenge of a setback, and figure out a way around it. Use setbacks as a stepping-stone to something better. Look at adversity as an opportunity to learn and grow and, thereby, take control. This doesn't mean you can control everything that happens to you. It means you can choose what you think about and how you react to what happens to you. Don't let 'blamer thinking' turn you into a victim.

You don't always get what you want

I heard a story about a little girl who prayed for a horse. Eventually, her mother asked if her prayer had been answered. The girl matter-of-factly replied, "Yes, the answer was No."

If your heart's desire is a person you will have to look elsewhere for advice, but if your heart's desire is a job, an opportunity, or work-related activity, then I have some suggestions. First of all, if our mission is to be the best we can be and help those around us be the best they can be, maybe making an idol out of any particular activity is not best for us. Opportunities are continually knocking at the door. Don't be blinded to the opportunity to grow and be of service, even if the opportunity doesn't appear to be your heart's desire. Sometimes we need to take what looks like a detour in order to be prepared for future challenges. Recognize opportunities of all kinds, and take advantage of them. After all, I didn't become a teacher. Instead, I became a Fellow, and teaching became a part of what I do.

Never underestimate the good you have already done. It will come back to bless you, but you may miss the blessing if you are too focused on a particular outcome. Several years ago, my sister-in-law contacted a local funeral home about providing biographical services to the families of their clients. The company decided not to go forward with the concept as presented, which disappointed her, however she recently attended a funeral there and discovered they had taken her concept and modified it, making it affordable. The service they provide gives the families a lasting reminder to help them through their period of grief, and my sister-in-law is thrilled with the result.

What if life is not perfect?

Along about high school I concluded that someday I would 'arrive'. I'd be wise enough not to create problems and smart enough to see trouble coming and somehow avoid it. Forty years later, I've given up expecting to have a perfect life. The big difference is that instead of seeing problems as something to fret over, I regard them as challenges and opportunities to learn and grow. I'll never be grown up, so how can I possibly 'arrive'?

In the spring of 2006, I was scheduled to attend a standards meeting in Geneva, Switzerland, as part of the US delegation. My air fare was non-refundable and the hotel was booked. To be a part of the US delegation to an ITU meeting, you must either attend a two-hour meeting in Washington DC or teleconference in. I teleconferenced. My company (that is to say, I) submitted three contributions, which were duly discussed at the meeting. Since the contributions were for information only, they were company positions rather than a US position.

Two weeks before the meeting, I received an e-mail informing me my name had been crossed off the delegation roster. Someone in the State Department or the White House had decided I should not attend as a US representative. I was stunned. I left a message for the person who runs the calls and had sent me the e-mail. I wanted to know "Why?" She left me a phone message urging me not to take it personally, and insisting the reasons would never be disclosed. She had pointed out in her email that my company was a 'sector member', and I could therefore attend the meeting as a representative of my company instead of a representative of my country.

I'd like to say I was undaunted, but I can't lie. As editor of the original JPEG standard, I'd requested half of one day out of the two-week meeting be devoted to discussions on future possible enhancements, so I needed to be there. After a few hours, I confirmed I could still participate in the next US meeting/call. I did attend the meeting in Geneva.

Sometimes life gives you lemons, and you won't always be able to make lemonade. Don't whine, "It's not fair." If someone promised you fair, they were mistaken. Pick yourself up, dust yourself off, and get on with life. Figure out what you can salvage from the situation, and learn from the experience. Next time.

Find your own style

Different people have different ways of dealing with setbacks. I have a friend who has a favorite saying when he hits an obstacle. He asks himself, and has been known to ask the obstacle, "Is it under, over, around, or through?" He is confident that within twenty-four hours he will be on the other side of the obstacle. He doesn't care if he tunnels under it, climbs over it, goes around it, or, if necessary, bulldozes through it. He quickly assesses which method will take the least effort and gets moving.

For my part, I find it helps to write down the pros and cons of taking action. Of course, I only do this for issues that appear to deserve action. Seeing things in black and white either moves me to act or convinces me action is unnecessary. Either way, I don't spend any more time fretting.

I also refuse to make major decisions without first praying about them and then sleeping on them. Prayer is a constant in my life. I don't always have a clear answer in the morning, but I get a good night's sleep. Often in the morning, I do know the answer.

Setbacks are an excellent opportunity to reconsider your goals. This doesn't always mean giving up on them. It may mean you want to learn to 'zig and zag'. Think of a sailboat. The boat tacks left and right as the fastest way to travel into the wind (against opposition). You can get around some obstacles by appearing to head temporarily in another direction and then heading back as soon as you are around the rocks. If your goals remain worthy and you remain passionate about them, use your problem solving skills to figure out how to accomplish them. The time when you face obstacles is a good time to enlist help from your mentors, both as advisers and as supporters.

Pretend, and see if you like the answer

Albert Einstein was once asked, "How to do you make decisions?" He responded, "I flip a coin." The questioner was amazed and asked, "You believe in luck?" Einstein answered, "No, I see if I like the answer." This story helps me. I don't actually flip a coin, but I arbitrarily pick a solution and mentally pretend I'm implementing it. I see what is involved. Sometimes I'll go for several days acting as if I have my answer without actually committing myself. I pretend.

I used this method when I thought I wanted to write computer-based physics curricula as my life-work. I contacted the College of Education and explored a Doctorate of Education. I went so far as to ask someone to be my thesis advisor. The potential advisor said, "Yes, but you are making a mistake. This is a one-way street. You will never be acceptable to a Physics department with a Doctorate of Education. With a Physics PhD, you can always choose to go into Education later. I think we can find you the funding, and I would be honored to be your advisor, but think carefully about it before making your final decision."

Before the end of the day, I went back to my original choice for a thesis advisor. I explained, "I can now get the computer to do whatever I want, but I don't know what I should have it do. Writing Physics course work will not help me know that. I've explored a Doctorate of Education and my potential advisor thinks it's a mistake. I agree. I am now ready to go into thesis research seriously. Will you be my thesis advisor?" I was taking a unit of independent research with his post-doc because, as I had explained six months before, "I want to know what I am training students for when I write physics courses for the computer." My advisor was pleased I was on a full-year Fellowship because he had an opening the next Fall when I would need funding again.

The Importance of Fallback Plans

You need to know what you will do if your plan goes awry. When I was young, my family went camping in the California Sierra Nevada Mountains almost every summer weekend. People frequently expressed shock that we didn't own a tent. I can still remember Dad's fallback plan, "We can drive home in less than three hours if it rains too hard to camp without a tent." That never happened.

Another example of a fallback plan comes to mind from the family trip to Alaska. Ten people headed north, packed into a

VW microbus. We carried one spare tire, but there was no room for a second spare. Before we left, someone asked Dad, "What will you do if you have a second flat before the first one is fixed?" He answered, "I'll just flag down the next VW and ask to borrow their spare tire until we get to a town where we can get the tires fixed and return their spare."

Sure enough, when we hit pavement after 1800 miles of the unpaved Alcan Highway in Canada without incident, we started having flats. Dad's fallback plan worked exactly the way he expected. I'm sure he would have come up with a solution to the problem, but having thought it out before hand meant he didn't have to fret about it.

Knowing your fallback plan keeps you from going into a tizzy if Plan A doesn't work. One of my mentees had to pass qualifying exams before she could enter the PhD program. Exams are not her favorite activity and she worried she might not pass them. When I told her my backup plan—that she could transfer to another university and keep going—she was not pleased. The threat of having to change schools made her more determined. She has completed the testing requirement.

When you don't have an alternate plan, it's like putting all your eggs in one bowl of cherries. Someone goes rooting around in the bowl looking for the perfect cherry, breaks the eggs, and spoils the cherries. You come to a complete stop if something goes wrong. You may find another plan based on the circumstances when Plan A becomes unfeasible, but having a fallback plan means you don't waste time. You have already recognized there is more than one way to skin a cat (one of Mom's favorite sayings).

What if you come in second, after working hard to be the best? Since life is a journey, not a destination, don't be discouraged. You never know what the future holds. There is no reason it will not be good. Sincerely congratulate the winner and move on to plan B. Surely, you have learned by now to have a plan B.

Sometimes the problem goes beyond fallback plans

Sometimes you try everything, and nothing works. This is the time to re-evaluate. Ask yourself, "Is this task or project important enough to spend time and energy on what looks like a hopeless task?" If the answer is "No," move on to a higher priority task. If the answer is "Yes," ask others for help and ideas. You may be approaching the problem from the wrong direction. Give yourself permission to stop hitting your head against a brick wall when you're going the wrong direction. Most problems can be solved when approached from the right direction.

A friend of mine accomplished his billion-dollar-plus passion by "tin cupping it around outside companies." Instead of continuing to butt his head against the brick wall of internal funding, he found companies who recognized the need for an order of magnitude improvement in chip speed at less power. Some of them bet their companies on his work being successful. It was. One of them invited him to their Corporate Technical Recognition Event as the first-time-ever outside speaker.

Unfortunately, sometimes we goof up big-time. I'm assuming no one died. If someone died, recovering is difficult, but putting your life on hold is never the solution. You need to be sure you have repented, expressed remorse, attempted to make amends, and learned from the experience. Then put it behind you and move on.

Rather than try to hide your mistakes, admit to them and figure out how to make amends. Enlist the help of your network, your friends, and mentors, to find a solution to the problem. Problems lose much of their power when you have friends working with you to find solutions and ways to correct the mistake. I can work with people who own up to mistakes quickly. I have trouble trusting people who try to hide their mistakes, or even worse, blame others for them.

According to Mom, "Fear is like a magnet; it attracts what you are afraid of." If you are afraid of consequences from a past poor decision, those consequences are likely to come about. Grow beyond your mistakes and quit hugging them to you. As you let go, you can forgive yourself and forget it. Mistakes don't continue to haunt your life when you have truly repented and been redeemed.

The desire to please everyone all the time is an impossible goal. It also hands manipulators the power to control you, and they will not have your best interests in mind. They will always find something negative to say. Do your own evaluation. Sometimes you have to remind yourself, the only power words have is the power you give to them. When someone says something hurtful, withhold that power and let negative evaluations starve for lack of notice. Many seeming setbacks occur to those who are 'people pleasers'. Don't allow disapproval to ruin a single day of your life.

Another company Fellow gave a talk on "How to make things happen in big corporations." He described his frustration as nay-sayers had tried to stop him doing what he needed to do. Later, these same pessimists claimed to have supported him all along. He urged us not to bother with revenge because, "Time wounds all heels." If you become obsessed with making someone else acknowledge your work, you give them power over you. You don't want that, so forgive, and let go.

When I went to live in Germany, my goal was to be a 'good German'. It was a wonderful experience, but no matter how hard I tried, I couldn't turn myself into a good German. Every time my German mother explained a difference between German and American customs, I took it as criticism. I vividly remember arriving for an excursion with the buttons on my coat unbuttoned. She explained it was the custom in Germany to button your coat buttons. Finally, I gave up. "They asked for an American, so they are going to get an American." Life was much more fun after that. I appreciated nuances without feeling like a failure because I hadn't noticed them before. No one else was trying to make me into a German, but my desire to please put me into a state where simple observations became criticisms.

Always consider the possibility of failure. Before I commit to a risky project, I consider the worst thing that can happen and have a plan in mind for handling it. By asking the questions, "What is the worst that can happen?" and "What is the best that can happen?" I mentally prepare myself to deal with the future. If I'm leading a team, I might ask the team these questions in order to line up better fallback plans. This is not a scare tactic; it's a matter of recognizing we have no guarantee of success. You will not always be successful. Preparing for the worst takes some of the terror out of failure.

Along the same lines, be prepared to declare failure when you think you have no chance of success. About a decade into my career, I made the conscious choice to kill my own projects. If you allow a doomed project to linger in agony, you waste time and resources. You also increase your frustration and stress levels unnecessarily. Cut your losses and move on. My team and I often decide what to do if we don't make our first milestone before beginning the project. Does initial failure represent a 'go/no go' decision or only a wake up call to try harder? We try to have a semi-successful attempt available for use if, in the end, we can't do better. This is particularly important if a product group is depending upon us. If we absolutely can't do better, at least we have something to give them.

Summary (including Introduction)

- Get at least five mentors
- Mentor at least five people
- Written goals help define your values and make decisions faster
- Expand your high impact work, and decrease your low impact work
- Regard setbacks as opportunities to grow and feature them in mentoring stories
- Fallback plans prepare to you continue moving forward after a disappointment.

2

The Softer Skills

*C*ommunication is critical to success in business. A vast amount of time is spent writing memos, presenting results, and talking to people in order to get the job done.

Presentation Skills

Surveys have found Americans are more afraid of public speaking than of death. As a seventh grader, I had to give a book report in class. My voice quavered and my knees shook. In high school, I took classes in public speaking and debate. One day I had an epiphany. I was tired of being scared, so I decided these were my friends and I'd concentrate on communicating with them instead of worrying what they were thinking. I've enjoyed public speaking ever since.

Mom came from a small town, but she took debate in high school. When she was elected PTA president, she memorized everything she had to say to run the first meeting in advance. Soon it got easier and she enjoyed being in charge. She encouraged us to get over our fear of speaking to groups. I remember times when my parents had us talk for five minutes at the dinner table on a topic picked by a sibling. I ran out of things to say about birds in one minute. My older sister talked for the entire time. It was a skill I wanted and decided to learn.

Mom pulled me out of honors English to take high school Debate. The guidance counselors didn't want honors students wasting their time on Debate because of the many weekend competitions, so they deliberately scheduled it to conflict with honors English. I have consciously used the analysis skills I learned in Debate in meetings I have attended. Recognizing the ways in which speakers try to manipulate their audiences is essential.

Graduate students give a seminar on their PhD topic for their 'prelim', the last step before embarking on the PhD research. When you finish your studies, you must defend your thesis. If you can enjoy the talk and the questions afterwards, the defense is much less stressful.

Essential skill for business

As a researcher, you will be expected to give talks. In Research, we gave department talks (sometimes as dry runs for conference presentations), conference talks, customer presentations, and so on. You will have opportunities to introduce speakers, give seminars at universities, and present your work at conferences.

Public speaking can and should be fun. Be prepared.

You won't always receive prior notice before you make a presentation. When I helped set the facsimile standard, I attended meetings in Geneva, Switzerland and Kyoto, Japan, in 1978 and 1979, respectively. Before the Geneva meeting, I carefully checked that I was not expected to give a presentation. During the meeting, the Japanese introduced their proposal in fifteen minutes. I wrote an outline of their introduction on the back of my tablet and then, during questions and answers, I filled in the figure numbers and page numbers from my proposal. I used the Japanese proposal as a template and substituted my information in appropriate places. Since the basic technology was close, the documents needed similar diagrams and format.

The experienced standards person in charge of my company delegation informed me during the break that I would have to make a presentation lasting *exactly* the same amount of time as the Japanese presentation. I flipped my tablet over and showed him the outline. I had never before done a talk with simultaneous translation. He had to slow me down so the translators could keep up. Then I realized I could faintly hear the translation leaking from the head sets and I used the translation time to think. Being able to say, "Now turn to Figure X on page Y" and have 150 delegates respond by turning to page Y, gave me a tremendous sense of power. My colleague warned me at the 3 minute, 30 second, and 5 second points, so I finished the presentation on time to the second. I could not have done so without years of experience in giving talks.

Practice really does make perfect, or at least better.

Know your audience

An important element in giving good talks is knowing your audience and understanding what they want and need. I learned the hard way to ask questions about the audience before accepting a speaking engagement. Normally, important presentations are scheduled weeks in advance, so when I received three days notice, it should have alerted me something was different, particularly since I was not allowed to decline. Stranger yet was my third line manager's advice during the dry run, "Just snow them." My talk on data compression opened with the "Status of CCITT fax proposal." My audience in the division president's conference room asked questions for a half hour before allowing me to move on to the second chart. I could see the division president with a slight smile on his face and, my third line manager with a big grin, so I didn't try to keep to the schedule. It was several days later before I realized this was part of a corporate audit initiated by another division who saw our tiny five-person research project as competition with their product. After that, I learned to ask questions about the purpose of a talk and the audience.

Be prepared to change your talk to fit the audience. As part of the facsimile standardization effort, I proposed to give all-day seminars in Europe. For the Paris seminar, I arrived a day early and did a dry run through my material. At the end of the day, I was told my material was for the wrong audience. I needed to start with basics. It took all night, but I had a morning of 'basics' ready to go the next day.

I could tell the industrialists who arrived were unsure what to expect. They had been invited by our head of delegation—a well respected man. When I started in on the basics, the audience relaxed and listened intently. On the way to lunch, I overheard the chair of the ad hoc that had selected the one-dimensional standard data compression tables say, "Now I finally understand Huffman coding." When the day ended about three o'clock, I knew I had successfully educated the audience about data compression and some of the differences between the competing proposals. I made no attempt to convert them to our view point. We wanted them to reach their own conclusions, but we wanted their conclusions to come from an educated view and not from politics.

If I had given my initial talk, the audience would have walked away confused and no better educated than when they sat down. While you should never 'talk down' to your audience, you must make allowances for their level of expertise. Your job is to educate, but without sufficient background information, your audience may not be able to learn.

Pat Heim talks and writes about her Dead-Even Power Rule. She wrote the book *Hardball for Women*. In it, she encourages women to take the initiative and always have an elevator speech ready. An elevator speech is of course, the thirty-second explanation of what you do.

You must understand the purpose of your talk if you are to teach people anything. Too often, we don't clearly define the intent. Sloppy thinking and planning leads to a poor talk. In marketing, I learned to start with the three written objectives I want the audience to remember. As you talk, repeat those objectives and make sure they come through clearly. If you plan your talk carefully, your audience will remember what you said.

Stop speech avoidance

If you have any hesitancy about public speaking, set a goal, and make a plan to get over it. Now. Take advantage of every opportunity to speak publicly and become comfortable with the experience before you sabotage your career by trying to avoid speaking to groups. Do you really want to go through your career terrified you might have to give a presentation? The more you succeed, the more likely you are to be asked to speak.

In Boulder, two of the developers I was mentoring were afraid of giving talks. I challenged both of them to get over it. In less than six months, by embracing opportunities to speak, both individuals were no longer afraid to make presentations. One became a superb speaker. I asked her how she felt after her first outstanding talk. She replied, "I got up there and realized I was the expert. I knew more about this field than they did. So I relaxed and enjoyed giving the talk." I've known several lousy writers to thrive, but never poor speakers.

One way to help yourself get beyond your fear of public speaking is to join Toastmasters. I first heard of Toastmasters because my first manager was encouraged to attend. His talks went from consistently poor to alternating between reasonable and brilliant in about a year. More recently I encouraged someone I was mentoring to join Blue Masters, the Boulder company Toastmasters Club. Later, another member told me if my mentee gives a presentation, the lunch room is packed. He has become a superb speaker. Toastmasters is one more way to network and allow others to help you.

Listening Skills

If you are not a good listener, eventually this weakness will become a derailer for your career. You cannot participate well in a team if you don't let everyone else participate. You need to *hear* what they say. Good listening skills are crucial for genuine leaders. As an added incentive, a recent article indicated those without good listening skills—those who interrupt rather than allowing others to finish their thoughts and sentences—are more likely to suffer from cardiovascular disease, heart attacks, high blood pressure, and strokes. They become too involved in themselves to allow others to participate and the stress kills them. As a test of heart disease, it appears to be more reliable than any medical tests available.

One good way to practice listening skills is to ask your relatives for their stories. And then listen. Some of them may consider themselves failures, so don't push too hard, but do encourage them when they want to talk. My grandmother

(Mom's mom) used to tell us the same old stories. As kids, we grew tired of hearing them. Then she traveled with us to Alaska for five weeks. She told new stories because she had time to think and remember what she had already told us.

Besides simply learning to do a better job of listening, you can learn some amazing things from and about your family by allowing the older generation to tell their stories. Mom's mom married a boyhood friend of Dad's dad. Dad was instrumental in the founding of the Sister Cities organization. Mom's mom helped institute a school breakfast program during the Depression. I once met the man who enabled the first night rescue of a downed fighter pilot from an aircraft carrier. Learning to listen can add a wealth of knowledge to your life.

While you are listening, be aware of your assumptions. A cousin first pointed out to me a new way to look at the word 'assume'. She wrote it on a napkin as ASS_U_ME. She explained it made an "ass out of you and me." Most of my boppers have come through the years because I assumed the wrong things. A bopper, by the way, is one of those incredibly stupid mistakes that make you bop yourself on the head and ask, "What was I thinking?"

Let it run awhile

I once attended a session on teaching that helped me be a better listener in all aspects of my life. The instructor used the analogy of taking your car to the shop for repairs. An expert mechanic doesn't start tinkering immediately. First, he lets the car run awhile and he listens. Only after he has identified the problem does he go to work. Don't start suggesting solutions before a person has had a chance to 'run awhile'. Sometimes a good listening ear is all the person needs. I know I sometimes just want a sounding board in order to figure out how to handle a problem myself. The solution you find yourself means more to you than the solution someone else gives you. Being a good listener allows you to be a good mentor.

Be aware of your assumptions, and examine them regularly. I used to visit the Research Laboratory on the opposite coast at least once a year where another group was also active in data compression. Their interests lay in hardware, whereas my team was optimizing for software speed. On one visit, I finally understood the problem was technical and not political. The entropy codec we were promoting would cost them a factor of two in throughput. Their method would slow down our software by a factor of two. Since, when the software ran out of steam we needed very high speed hardware, this situation was not acceptable. That night I invented the solution. Learn to listen carefully to contrary views, and check your assumptions sooner. Who knows how much time we wasted simply because we didn't listen to each other? Good listening skills require you to put aside your preconceptions.

Body Language

If you want to thrive in a world-wide corporation, you need to recognize the significance of the body language we read and the signals we send. There are several good books available addressing body language. I encourage you to check out your local library and read at least three. Since the signals do not remain the same throughout the world, you should refresh your studies before traveling too far.

If you are listening carefully, make sure your body language conveys that information. Restlessness is a sign of impatience or disagreement. Sometimes it helps to explain why you are sending contrary signals. At the end of the day, when I am completely relaxed, I yawn. This doesn't mean I'm bored, it just means I'm comfortable and relaxed. If I explain to my host and hostess what the yawning means, they won't think I'm not enjoying my visit.

Most books indicate that a relaxed posture, with the arms open, indicates receptiveness. Closed fists or crossed arms indicate defensiveness, disbelief, and internal turmoil. For many cultures, refusing to make eye contact is a sign of misdirection, but for other cultures, it is a sign of modesty.

I read an article about a school principal who expelled a Hispanic girl because she wouldn't look him straight in the eye. He read that as a sign of guilt. Fortunately, one of the counselors was aware that for her to look him in the eye would be considered bold and inappropriate. The counselor intervened and corrected the injustice. In Japan, I picked up some wildly humorous books on cultural differences, including body language. Listen, observe body language, and when in doubt, ask.

In June 2002, Debra Benton spoke at a seminar on "How to Think Like a CEO." It was a career-changing event for me. Ms. Benton explained that more than 85% of communication is nonverbal (body language). Most of us are not good enough actors to hide our true thoughts. You know when you start a discussion with someone whether they approve of you or are hostile. Debra explained that what we think about ourselves and about the person we are talking to is communicated in subtle ways.

She had concrete suggestions on projecting a professional presence that doesn't sabotage our professional goals. She illustrated her recommendations with short skits. Would you prefer to follow a slouching, frowning engineer or a commanding (i.e. good posture), confident engineer? She spent time exposing thought habits and patterns that inhibit career growth—like waiting for someone else to make the first move instead of introducing yourself to those around you. Her suggestions are contrary to many female cultural expectations. We all know dogs establish the order of the pack through nonverbal communication. What if humans have equivalent behavior but are largely unaware of it? Those with good role models learn to assert their position, while others wonder why nobody listens to them.

Ms. Benton's books are not as effective as watching her demonstrations, but they are worth reading. The first one is *Lions Don't Need to Roar: Using the Leadership Power of Professional Presence to Stand Out, Fit In, and Move Ahead.* This book covers most of what she illustrated in her seminar. The second is *How to Think Like a CEO: The 22 Vital Traits You Need to Be the Person at the Top.* To my astonishment, the things that make me unique and make me enjoy my work are not things I have to give up. Of the twenty-two traits, the one I need to work on most is number six: Thinking before Talking.

After hearing Debra speak, I understood why during my undergraduate physics classes I had observed a group of guys surround the only other female in the class to tell her she did not belong in physics. I waited for the same thing to happen to me, but it never did. As I described this to a friend, I instinctively gathered myself together into a strong posture position. I wasn't going to let anyone talk me out of physics. If you don't look like you mean it, why should anyone believe you?

In addition to our body posture sending the signal "Don't mess with me," humor can diffuse many situations. It is useful to have a few sentences pre-canned to use in situations where your body language is not enough. The one I use occasionally is, "And your tickets to the moon are in the mail." It is similar to suggesting, "If you believe that, I have this bridge in Brooklyn to sell you." It's okay to wink at someone, but you have to keep a straight face while doing so.

Humor is different from sarcasm. Humor aims to get *everyone* laughing together. It doesn't single someone out to be laughed at, hurt, or wounded. I remember hearing the following example of using humor to solve a problem many years ago. An African-American was transferred to an all white military base before the military was well integrated. When he walked into the mess hall, the hostility was tangible. Instead of feeling hurt or afraid, after a pregnant pause he boomed forth in his best British accent, "I say ol' chaps, surely you're not going to hold it against me that I have a better tan than you?" The hall exploded with laughter and the hostility vanished.

Negotiating

I remember my first trip to Rome. Dad asked how to pronounce Italian numbers every chance he got. Then we went to a local market. He and the vendor enjoyed a half-hour negotiation in Italian supplemented with hand waving. Dad picked up a pair of leather gloves. When he had a final price, he added a second pair of gloves and continued to negotiate a new price for both. Once that was settled, he picked up another pair of gloves and continued the process. Both of them had a ball creating drama over gloves. Dad walked away once, but the vendor called him back. When we left, Dad had three pairs of gloves.

We all negotiate many times a day, sometimes with ourselves, sometimes with others. Every time we set a meeting time, change a meeting time, or arrange for events with more than one person we are negotiating. The process of reaching a consensus when the starting point includes disparate positions is negotiation. In some cultures, negotiation is a national pastime. Vendors expect the price to be negotiated downward and they feel cheated if you accept their first offer. However, once having arrived at an acceptable price, you buy now or never. You don't walk away, then come back an hour later and expect to buy at your previously negotiated price. The vendor may refuse to sell to you at all. In other cultures, the price is the price. Few of us can imagine going into Bloomingdale's and negotiating the price on a new dress.

There are multiple negotiating styles. One common style, which I am pleased to observe is becoming less popular, is "I can win if you lose." Some people need to win at the expense of those around them. This style of negotiating invariably leads to bad feelings on the part of the loser. The loser will often seek revenge. You only have to read what happened after World War I to realize the consequences of having a clear 'loser'.

Another style is to arrive at the best possible compromise. This is a common strategy when the sides are evenly matched. Each side attempts to optimize its gains, but does not expect to end up with all the gains. One of the mottos for standards committee compromises was 'Equal pain'. Each side shared equally in the losses. This is based on the assumption that the pie is of fixed size. If one side gets a larger piece, the other side must end up with a smaller piece.

The best negotiating style is 'win/win'. Replace 'equal pain' with 'equal gain'. Each side wants both sides to come out ahead. Sometimes just challenging everyone to find 'the third answer' is sufficient to release the creativity needed to look beyond compromise solutions that only include the starting points and find a solution that provides a win for everyone. If you regard the starting points as the base of a triangle, then the third answer is a point above the base. 'Win/win' requires you to assume there is enough good to go around instead of a limited, fixed amount. My first manager said, "Rather than fighting over the bones of a too small pie, let's figure out how to create a bigger pie." You can read more about win/win negotiating in Stephen R. Covey's *The 7 Habits of Highly Effective People*. Practice it. It works.

Occasionally you will meet someone who prefers 'lose/lose' situations where nobody wins. Be cautious. If you find a winning answer, this extreme pessimist will unconsciously look for a way to sabotage the solution. Unable to accept any good, the person who is more comfortable losing will block progress by planting fears and expecting the worst. Only time and experience will tell you if an individual is able to accept progress and is trying to help by playing the devil's advocate, or if they truly expect the worst from life.

Some people like to argue. Don't be sucked into justifying yourself or your ideas with one of these people. When I first started work, I met someone whose first answer was always "No." He expected you to argue to change his mind. He enjoyed verbal debate, was exceedingly talented, and usually won the argument. The effect of talking to him was a wet blanket on the fire of new and creative ideas. Since most research is a dead-end, he was more often right than wrong, but no one will ever know how many brilliant ideas he killed with his superb verbal sklls. If you meet someone like this, do not share your ideas in their infancy. Wait until you can support them.

It has been said, we under-value the concessions made by others in a negotiation by a factor of two, and over-value our own concessions by a factor of two. When all parties have good intentions, there is a mismatch in perceived concessions by a factor of four. When the mismatch is bigger than four, negotiations are not necessarily being done in good faith.

If you don't enjoy negotiating, think about taking a class. Reading books can also help. As well as writing the book and publishing audio versions, Covey's organization teaches classes on the *7 Habits*. It may be worth your while to look into the classes. Failing to learn negotiating skills will handicap your life and your career.

Don't be gullible

Dad's dad was a great teaser, so when Grandmother had a candy bowl filled with "fancy white gravel" he insisted it was found in Nature. My best friend heard a lot about that "gravel" which looked exactly like the rocks in her driveway. I convinced her she should test the stones in her driveway. Now, my grandfather had told me you couldn't wash the stones or they would vanish, so my friend tested the cleaner stones from the edges of the drive with her teeth. After several unsuccessful tests, I realized Granddad had fooled me again. Even at eight years old, I should have known better.

When someone tells you something that doesn't seem right, don't just swallow it. Do your research. With the internet, it's relatively easy to verify known facts. If your research indicates the information you received was correct, you know you can trust that person. When you discover you have met a person who enjoys fooling people, keep it in mind. Everything they say becomes suspect. When you know the person you are negotiating with is less than perfectly honest, you are in a better position to negotiate.

He who has the pen rules

I heard the phrase "he who has the pen rules" soon after becoming involved in the JPEG standard. If you are the person who documents discussions and writes up neutral minutes, your interpretation of what happened becomes the starting point. Always represent conclusions fairly, or the group will change your minutes, and you will lose your position of power.

Once, I attended a standards meeting as a last minute substitute. This group had a culture of contention and difficult negotiations. Early in the meeting, I presented my company's proposal. I could tell many of the objections were knee jerk reactions, not actual responses to the proposal, so I dramatically raised the transparency marker and declared, "He who has the pen rules." Then with a long, slow bow, I extended the pen to the most vocal critic and continued, "So I present you with the pen." With power comes responsibility. My critic was now in a position to work. I sat down and worked on cutting and pasting diagrams. For the next hour, I gave the impression I wasn't interested in the discussion. Since I was not fighting, the other side abruptly conceded and accepted our proposal without change.

At one meeting, another company claimed they had a better proposal than ours. They made a lot of noise about it, and claimed it was patent free. The regular standards person told me their proposal had never been formally submitted to the standards body. The rep from the other company kept hovering around our discussions, so I made a point of suggesting he join us. Then I learned his company would not be present at the standards meeting the next day. As a rule of thumb, if a company is not represented, its proposals are dropped. After some internal debate, I blurted out, "Do you know your company's proposal has never been submitted and if no one attends, it will not be considered?" He replied, "Yes. The proposal has accomplished its purpose; to get everyone to agree to fee-free licensing." He negotiated what he wanted without ever having to enter into negotiations.

One thing I learned from my first standards meeting is that you can't negotiate technically alone. It is impossible to talk and listen at the same time. One person needs to pay attention to the opposition while the other is talking. My hardware colleague attended the standards meeting in Kyoto so we could trade off taking the lead in negotiations.

Find your negotiating style

Not too long after a negative interaction with a secretary, I read a book about negotiating which claimed copying male styles often backfires for females. Since all facets of your work life involve negotiation, you should select one or more managers of your sex who seem to be consistently successful in their negotiations. Ask them for mentoring advice and coaching. Find the style that works best for you. My style includes prayer for inspiration and listening for answers to my prayers.

It took two weeks to negotiate a valid compromise solution at the November fax standards meeting in Kyoto, but I think most people went home satisfied with the compromise. The final algorithm was 'good in hardware and software'. The President of the Research Division described my experience as, "Joan snatched partial victory from the jaws of sure defeat."

When I went to Kyoto, I was no longer oblivious to national cultures, so I had realized it might be awkward for me to negotiate in Japan. In reality, I think my gender gave me an edge. The male negotiators weren't sure how to deal with me, and that put them off their stride. No one in my company brought the issue up before I went to the meeting, but in the week after I returned I counted sixteen phone calls asking me, "Did it matter that you were a woman?" I was proud my company had expected me to take the lead. My hardware colleague had been prepared to take over if necessary, but instead we were able to tag-team. One took the lead while the other listened and thought. When the lead got tired, the other took over. Another lesson learned. You don't have to do it all yourself.

Always go into a negotiation knowing what you define as success. Knowing what success is makes it easier to avoid being caught up in debate. Success may be something as simple as planning a meeting at a time that does not conflict with other commitments or it may be something as important as a standard good in hardware and good in software. If you practice on the little things, the bigger things become easier.

Learn from your experiences. Ask a good friend to critique your negotiating style. You will know you have found your own unique style when it comes naturally and effortlessly. Observe others and incorporate the best of what you see.

Writing Skills

Mom insisted we take typing in high school. If we typed 40 words a minute (even just once), we were given a portable manual typewriter to take with us to college. I remember hearing another mother self-righteously declare she would never let her daughters learn to type, so they couldn't ever be secretaries. My reaction was horror.

In today's world, everyone does their own typing. Programming skills are essential to scientists and engineers, and programming involves typing. Most working people spend more than 30 percent of their time writing. All my mentees type. If you don't, learn how.

Writer's block is no excuse

My high school English teacher assured me that English PhDs were hired to write technical papers for scientists. Because I believed her, I didn't work on getting rid of writer's block. I also didn't work on the elements of structure in a paragraph, a paper, or a book. I can stare at a blank piece of paper for hours. If you want to succeed, you must learn to communicate in writing.

One solution to my writer's block problem was to pretend my paper was a talk. This idea came to me my sophomore year while attending Stanford-in-England. I created an entire paper as a talk, practiced until I had it memorized, and then wrote it out. I was unwilling to waste a three-day weekend struggling to compose the paper longhand. Instead, I explored England.

Research is pointless unless you can communicate your results to other people. A cure for cancer that never leaves the laboratory won't save anyone's life. Research on the causes and cures for autism don't affect the world until the paper is written and read.

Early on, I often did the first drafts for a team effort. My colleagues said harsh things about my disorganized papers, but they generally kept my paragraphs intact and rarely touched figures or tables. The final papers were much improved, but the experience didn't encourage me to enjoy writing. Meanwhile, I'd figured out that those English PhDs were not to be found. So I set a goal to get over my writer's block.

There is a correlation between trying to impress someone with complex writing, and trouble. When you compose a memo to communicate information, the writing flows. You don't waste time searching for the perfect, little known word, and you don't try to create complex sentences. You simply give the information you need to give. If you have issues with writing papers, try writing memos instead. Keep it simple. If necessary, you can fill in additional data on the second draft.

A book on writing had recommended keeping a daily diary, written longhand, on four by six cards. The process helps organize your thoughts, and makes writing a more natural process. I enjoyed waking up each morning and writing at least one side about what I had done the day before. The cards make writing letters easy, as well. You won't forget to include bits of news you intended to pass along. If you have issues with writing, try this method.

Trying to edit and compose simultaneously can lead to difficulties. The result is neither well-composed, nor well-edited. Make the effort to compose only. It helps to wait a day before rearranging and editing. For a paper, a week's wait is better. Once you have a complete draft, put the paper aside until you can read what is written instead of what you intended to write. My sister-in-law swears by this, although she admits after she's up to draft three or four, she begins to see what she thought she wrote instead of what's on the page in front of her.

Ask for help. It doesn't matter where you work, someone around you is an outstanding writer. When you've taken your paper as far as you think you can, ask them to read it. It is less painful to have them catch typos or point out awkward sentences than to have your colleagues rip into your papers. Sometimes just a few words can help you understand where you have gone wrong in the writing. If you do a lot of writing, consider joining—or forming—a writer's group. Rule number one in any writer's group is "No blood on the floor." Criticism must be constructive, pertinent, and phrased in such a way that the writer does not feel attacked.

One of my favorite fiction authors suggests creating a fifteen word outline. Many of us never learned how to outline properly. This new type of outline opens with a subject, action verb, and a direct object to state the problem. The last line is the subject (better be the main character), action verb, and a direct object giving the resolution. The three lines in between are three attempts to solve the problem. Start writing with the plot (structure) firmly in place. This was my personal epiphany.

Spend half your time figuring out the purpose of your paper, then fit a good strong beginning to a matching good strong ending before filling in the middle. This method forces you to decide the purpose of the paper and identify your target audience. When those two things are clear, the rest is easy. I often create my first draft with the subsections labeled from the three word lines. Later, I replace them with scientific terminology.

One of my earliest goals was to be an IBM Fellow. The only Fellows I knew had written books—and not just any old books, but classic reference books. So I set a goal to write a book on JPEG. There's no doubt we needed the book to explain the standard. When asked if I would join with my co-editor in writing an article for the ISO Standards Bulletin announcing and explaining the JPEG standard, I jumped at the chance.

I started with a fifteen word outline. I only remember the first and last lines: "World needs standard...JPEG establishes standard." From my outline, I worked each morning on one section. Each day I had a great sense of accomplishment. Sometimes I edited previous sections rather than working on new sections. This time when I gave my co-author my drafts, there was no reorganization to do. I had learned to plan an article.

Many of the engineers I worked with in Burlington were oblivious to the need to share their results and write technical papers, so I organized a special issue of the Research and Development Journal. About half the authors were novices. When they admitted they were struggling, we sat down together and created fifteen word outlines. Once they had the outline, they could write a good first draft of a paper in about a week. It was easy to figure out where the paper needed expansion and to convert the section headings from three words into appropriate technical jargon based upon the contents of the section. The official editor of the Research and Development Journal said he had never had so many papers arrive as good drafts. He only had minor touch up to do before publishing the papers.

Writing is an essential skill in business. If you have difficulty communicating through writing, try one of the methods outlined above. Write memos, and then expand them as necessary. Write on four by six cards so you can shuffle and organize more easily. Don't try to compose and edit at the same time. Take some time off from your paper between composing and editing. Ask for help from more competent writers. Try the fifteen word outline. If none of this works for you, go the library and check out writing books. Writing is not optional.

Appearance

We live in a litigious society. Neither your manager nor your official mentor is likely to say to you, "John, you dress like a refugee from a rock concert," "Mary, your skirts are too short," or "Sandra, you apply your make-up with a trowel." To say those things would subject your manager or mentor to legal action. On the other hand, people look at you. They form opinions about you. The opinions other people form can have an adverse effect on your career.

Dress for success (or not)

Some of you remember the 'dress for success' advice of the 80's. It turned me off.

However, I attended a seminar in which the instructor pointed out that a few good business suits made of durable material could simplify your life. I bought my first business suits. It worked.

Fortunately, we are past the time when dressing for success means wearing a basic blue or black suit at all times. Today we express our individuality in our style of dress, our hairstyle, and our make-up. But we still have to conform to company dress codes and standards of good taste, though those standards vary by company and national culture.

Every professional should own at least one conservative business suit. If your company subscribes to business casual, you may never wear your suit to work, but you must have it in your closet for emergency situations. You may be called upon to give a formal presentation. You may need to attend a funeral. You may have dinner with clients, or the boss.

I had an employee who had never appeared at the office in a suit. When he was scheduled to make a formal presentation at a conference, I had concerns. He assured me a business suit was not a problem, but I wondered what it would look like. Fortunately, he showed up in a very proper dark business suit—he played in an orchestra in his off hours.

A good way to determine the proper style of dress for your company is to look at what others are wearing. If tattered blue jeans and band tee-shirts are the order of the day, dressing too far 'up' from that standard won't help you advance your career. You should attempt to dress a little better than your peers, and not quite as well as your manager. If your manager consistently wears suits to work, you should do so as well. If khakis and knit shirts are the uniform adopted by everyone else, you should wear khakis, and perhaps a woven shirt. Leaders set new standards, and they set them higher than the previous standards. This is true in style of dress as well as in activities that are more important.

Wear clothing that allows you to present a professional image and fits the kind of work you do. Pretty dresses with long flowing skirts and multiple layers of ruffles may be your thing, but if they create a hazard in the workplace, you should find other places to wear them. My sister-in-law loves this style and would wear nothing else except for the fact she rolls over her skirts every time she moves her chair. Having her skirt tear away from the waistband and hang in tatters around her ankles doesn't present the romantic image she wants. Catching a sleeve in your equipment can be dangerous as well as making you look foolish.

Shoes should be sensible for the work you do, and dressy enough to present the image you need to present. My sister-in-law is a shoe collector. She owns at least three-dozen pairs of foolish, open-toed mules. Most companies frown on open-toes, and I always wonder how she manages to keep them on her feet, to say nothing of the hazards of walking around with your toes exposed to falling objects. Jimmy Choo's may be just right for Madison Avenue, but they don't work well in the lab or the boardroom.

If clothes aren't your thing

There are people in the world who consider shopping a recreational sport. I don't understand it, but have learned to appreciate them anyway. If you consider shopping a fate worse than death, take advantage of one of these misguided souls. They can be depended upon to tell you, "That style doesn't suit you," or, "That color doesn't work for you." Upscale department stores have professional shoppers who will select a number of outfits for you, including the necessary accessories. You simply show up, try on three or four selections, and purchase what works for you without the agony of shopping. I took advantage of this service when I attended the award dinner where the JPEG and MPEG standards received an engineering Emmy.

Some of us have no color sense, while others can tell at a glance whether two colors work well together. Have you ever seen someone dressed all in green? But the greens don't work together? Or varying shades of black? Some of us don't seem to realize black isn't just black. I can see it in my work. I can tell instantly in printing when something isn't right. But in clothes? Some of us don't notice when we, or someone else, is wearing mismatched colors. But there are many who do notice, and they form an unconscious opinion of us based on our clothing. Colors that don't work together, or styles that don't suit our body-types indicate sloppiness to these people, and that's an attitude we don't want to project.

My brother is color challenged. As far as he can tell, green is green. A few years back, his manager mentioned she could always tell when his wife went out of town. When she's home, she selects his shirt and tie to match his suit and he always appears at the office looking well dressed. When she's away, he finds a shirt, a tie, and a suit, but they invariably clash. He finally learned he can only wear combinations previously selected by his wife. If you are similarly challenged, ask your significant other to assist in your wardrobe selection. If you have no significant other, or if they have no color sense, ask the sales person (or professional shopper) at your favorite clothing store to pull together coordinated selections for you. Life will be easier when you don't have to worry about inconsequentials.

If you have no interest in outer appearances, my goal is not to teach you to care about such things above all else. But you should learn enough about color matching and style to present a well-groomed appearance. Either learn, or find someone else who can help you.

Cosmetics, necessary or superfluous?

Make-up is another issue for women. How much is too much? How little is too little? For my part, none is fine. I haven't seen a company dress code requiring female employees to wear make-up since the airlines stopped requiring stewardesses to wear a size eight and always be perfectly made-up and coiffed. I've never seen a man go to work with blue eye-shadow, black eyeliner, and red spots on his cheeks. Some women like make-up, and that's a personal choice. I would only warn you, make-up should be understated. If you think you may be wearing too much, you probably are. My sister-in-law speaks of women wearing 'half their body-weight' in make-up. Too much looks tawdry and cheap and can prevent you from achieving the promotions you deserve.

Hairstyle is a very personal matter.

Hairstyle used to be simple for men, and to a large extent, it still is—neat and clean. The length is largely dependent upon the type of work you do and the image you want to present. Most salesmen find it's advantageous to wear their hair conservatively—it doesn't offend their clients. Rock stars tend to wear long hair, frequently with spikes and colors to set them apart from the ordinary. Military men always wear their hair close-cropped. Long hair, mullets, braids, spikes, and unnatural colors convey varying degrees of rebellion. It's okay to convey rebellion, as long as you know you are doing so. Look around you. If the hairstyles worn by your colleagues are consistently either too conservative or too outlandish for your taste, you may be working in the wrong place. Make yourself comfortable. Comb-overs are always a mistake. They make you look desperate.

A good stylist will cut your hair to fit your face, but also to fit your image. This is truer for women than for men. If you want to present a severe image, obviously a fluffy cap of riotous curls doesn't work. Think about well-known actresses and the characters they play. Their stylists work hard to design 'do's' which will evoke certain images for the public. Imagine a woman with long flowing hair falling halfway to her waist in waves of flame red. How old is she? What's she wearing? What is her profession? If you're like most people, you pictured the heroine in a romance novel. Now imagine a woman with pale blond hair tucked neatly into a chignon. I'm seeing a woman somewhat older than our heroine, and someone with a businesslike attitude. What about the woman with silvery white hair in a halo of tight little curls around her head? Your grandmother, right? She's sweet and loving and always smells of chocolate chip cookies. The point is, people form opinions of you without ever having met you. You need to make certain those images are accurate ones. Your hairstyle is part of your image.

Everything I've said here has to do with style, and despite the adage "Image is everything," substance is more important. Make sure your 'style' reflects who you are, because other people will make assumptions based on what they see. If they see clothing or make-up more suited to the boudoir than the boardroom, they'll assume you don't belong. If they see colors that should never appear together, they'll assume you don't care. Once they get to know you, your substance will come shining through, but if your style puts them off, they won't make the effort to know you.

Social Graces

Our colleagues hold the key to our ultimate success. It is vital to create a support network. The 'support network' is what you create over time when you practice the social graces. I've noticed almost all higher level people know how much little courtesies count, and yet I don't ever remember being coached on them after I left home.

Table manners are even more important than your mother told you.

When I was growing up, the family always ate dinner together. It wasn't a matter of choice or convenience; this was family time. We gathered around the dinner table and talked about the events of the day. My sister-in-law's mother kept up a constant litany of, "Chew with your mouth closed. Don't talk with your mouth full. Keep your fingers out of your food. Use your knife and fork. Put your napkin in your lap. Use your napkin, not your sleeve." As a child, I didn't understand the importance of table manners. Then I entered the corporate world and found myself dining with people who didn't know and love me.

My sister-in-law tells a story about a cousin of hers. His parents weren't as assiduous as mine were in instilling the need for proper table manners. When he sat down to the table, he leaned down to his plate and shoveled the food into his mouth, chewing open-mouthed and talking freely as the mood struck him. Needless to say, no one wanted to sit across the table from him.

It wasn't until he was in college that he finally understood the problem. He went to dinner at his girlfriend's home, and true to form, when he sat down to the table he leaned forward and began shoveling the food into his mouth. His girlfriend and her parents sat back and stared, aghast. Finally, he realized how put off they were by his behavior, and how unusual it was. On his next trip home from college, he insisted his parents begin remedial training for his younger sister. He never wanted her subjected to the same sort of humiliation.

In recent years, many families have abandoned the habit of dining together each evening. Many young adults have never had the experience of dining with someone who insisted on proper table manners. Fortunately, it's never too late to learn. If you didn't learn as a child, learn now. Chew with your mouth closed. Don't talk with your mouth full. Keep your fingers out of your food. Use your knife and fork. Put your napkin in your lap. Use your napkin, not your sleeve. Practice at home, so when you dine out with those who don't know and love you, you won't embarrass them or yourself. If they see table manners more suited to the campfire than the dining room, they'll assume you have sloppy personal habits—and perhaps sloppy work habits as well.

Remember names

Knowing a person's name is a way of saying, "I care about you." As a freshman at Stanford University, I heard about the men's frosh-dorm Head Resident Assistant. He knew the names and home towns of all the men in his dorm before they arrived. He did about two weeks of evening drills from flash cards to memorize all 800 incoming students using pictures in the frosh book. On arrival day, he could welcome each newcomer by name as he introduced himself. The guys knew he could tell them apart. They felt welcomed and they respected him.

For decades, I believed I couldn't remember names, so I didn't try. Then, Robert Heinlein's book *Double Star* started me thinking in another direction. His main character, a down-on-his-luck actor, steps in for a kidnapped politician. The politician kept notes on his interactions with people, so the imposter—with copious help from the politician's staff—could fake it convincingly. Another Heinlein book, *Citizen of the Galaxy* had a young orphan training to become a spy. The spy-master taught him various memory tricks. *GMP: The Greatest Management Principle in the World* recommends keeping notes on customers, vendors, and important people for review before your next visit. Sales people and politicians use tools. I learned to do the same.

A retired General Manager once told me, "People won't tell you a problem if you are not on a first name basis." This made sense to me, because I would certainly hesitate to enter a superior's office if they didn't know who I was. My friend walked the plant twice a day, and looked for changes in behavior. If Joe's usual response to, "How are things?" was "Fine", then "Okay, I guess" was a good reason to pause and take a few extra moments to see if more information would be forthcoming.

One management course I took claims 'a crisis is a problem you didn't see coming'. Get to know your people so problems don't blindside you. Notice changes in behavior and changes in responses. If you see a problem coming, take action before it has time to become a crisis. Some people will never tell you directly when something's wrong in their life. If you think there's a problem, you might check with their best friend to see if he will tell you what's going on.

When I became the US Head of Delegation (HOD) to JPEG, one of my responsibilities was to run the US meetings. At the end of a sequence of meetings, I created the delegation roster. To do this, I needed to know names, spellings, and company affiliations. This is when I decided to do something about my memory. I ordered "Memory Made Easy" by Robert L. Montgomery from an IEEE flyer. I estimate my retention of names went from about 10% to about 50% after completing the course.

Don't go through your career handicapped by a lazy memory. There are numerous courses available to help you train yourself to remember names. Get one of them and study it. Failing to remember a person's name tells them you don't care about them. That's an attitude you never intend to convey.

Half the battle in remembering names is hearing (or in my case seeing) the names in the first place. Business cards are a life saver. Collect cards from everyone you meet, and of course introduce yourself and give them your card. Review the cards repetitively while looking at the person so the name and the face become connected in your mind. That way, the next time you meet that person, you won't stand there feeling like an idiot because they look familiar, but the name escapes you.

Reaching out (networking)

It is important to introduce yourself to others. Women and newcomers often believe they should hold back and not be too bold, but in business, making sure everyone is introduced to everyone else is considered taking the initiative. This holds true for both men and women. Be prepared to remember names. Handing out a business card will usually get one back. You can't leverage your contacts to solve problems until you create a network.

Take a few minutes to help newcomers learn about your community, both at home and at work. A friend recently told me her method for enjoying a social event where she doesn't know anyone, and may not have common interests with the other attendees. She looks around until she finds someone who looks even more miserable and uncomfortable than she feels. Then she makes it her mission to ensure that person enjoys the party. In the process, she meets other people, learns new things, and frequently makes good friends. A stranger is someone you haven't turned into a friend. Make the effort to befriend strangers. One of them will turn into an important contact later on.

Thank yous

Standards meetings taught me the importance of always thanking the meeting hosts. A formal resolution is put into the minutes. Usually, the meeting coordinators are invited into the room, the resolution is read, and everyone claps loudly to express their appreciation. Then the meeting adjourns. It seems like a small thing, but imagine if you had put in hours and hours of work on a project and nobody bothered to notice.

Belated thank yous may be even more important than the ones that come on time. While my aunt and I drove in the Palo Alto area, I told her stories from my frosh seminar with Dr. George Polya. His weekly class enabled me to take physics out of order and survive. Twenty years later, I was still talking about him, so my aunt said, "Why don't you stop and thank him in person?" The phone book gave us his address and we called to ask if we could stop by. My aunt talked to his wife while he showed me a wall of bound reprints (of his work) in multiple languages. At ninety-five, Dr. Polya was still active and read the mathematics literature daily.

Saying thank you takes so little effort.

Congratulations

My company usually organizes a folder of congratulatory letters for people hitting twenty-five years with the company, and another for retirement. Until I received my twenty-five year folder, I often failed to write letters except for close personal friends. As I flipped through my folder, I was astonished and touched by the many letters I received. I also realized the short letters with simple words were as touching as the long and detailed letters. Once I realized the importance of those notes, I started responding to letter requests more often.

Don't wait twenty-five years to understand the importance of congratulating someone on a job well done. If your company has a similar program, start responding now. Since you've learned to write, you can come up with a series of appropriate letters. Then as the occasion demands, you add a short personal note. It doesn't have to be a burden, and it will make a difference to the person you congratulate.

Whenever you hear of something worthy of congratulations, such as election to IEEE Fellow or National Academy of Engineering, make a point of sending a one or two sentence e-mail with a subject line of Congratulations. I blind copy my distribution list and note the copy in the e-mail. It's fun to spread the good news. Almost always, I get an e-mail back thanking me—a sign the person has learned the importance of saying, "Thank You."

Roasts

Roasts are an opportunity for public speaking, and an opportunity to say thank you. When my thesis advisor retired from the University of Illinois, his thesis students were invited to his retirement party and most came, including several from England. The invitation indicated there would be five minutes per person for individual comments. On the plane, I decided to try to give my first light-hearted talk so I made some notes on four by six cards. Part of the trick to giving a light-hearted talk is the pregnant pauses. For example, "I used to think he was omniscient because he always seemed to know to come by the lab when I was stuck, [pause] until I discovered the red spelling corrections in my lab book."

Years later, the Physics Department invited me to be their Physics Honors Luncheon speaker. I assumed my thesis advisor was behind the idea. In fact, he was out of town and knew nothing about it, but someone remembered my five minutes of comments at the retirement dinner and recommended me. I started to put together a technical talk. Fortunately, I called my sister-in-law who quickly corrected me, "Joan, this is a dinner speech. Technical talk will be deadly dull. Make it light-hearted." I did.

Meanwhile, I arranged a technical talk for the next day and could announce it for those who were interested. I was impressed with the equipment and the students (eager to learn) so seven months later I came back to teach for a semester which just shows how doing the right thing—in this case speaking up at my thesis advisor's roast—can result in good things happening. I was on leave of absence and I needed the opportunity to teach.

Of course, none of this would have happened without networking.

Condolences

Many of us tend to hide our heads when someone dies. We don't know what to say. Sometimes you can find an appropriate sympathy card, but then you feel guilty because it's not personal. When Mom passed on, I received many e-mail condolences. Even though I never responded, they helped. That's when I realized it doesn't matter what you say, it only matters that you care enough to say something. So this is a belated, "Thank you from my whole heart" for all those e-mails I never responded to.

Be prepared to participate in memorial services when an opportunity arises. Having learned to enjoy giving presentations, there is no barrier to the sharing and it helps. Unless you were particularly close to the deceased, keep your remembrances short. Be aware that stories are often shared further, and help heal the grief even for those who do not attend. An uncle passed on a few years ago, and my brother told me about the service. Three groups shared stories about him: relatives, his friends from work (who were also were also his hunting and fishing buddies), and Alcoholics Anonymous (AA) friends. My uncle had been sober for 55 years and faithfully attended Wednesday noon AA meetings for most of that time. His son had never seen him drink. My cousin closed the sharing time by thanking people and explaining he had not known the impact his father had by encouraging others to stay sober.

At Mom's memorial service, I told the story of strawberry crumpets. On a hot summer day, we were packing for a back-pack trip. The butter had to remain in the refrigerator because otherwise it would melt. Dad kept reminding Mom, and she assured him the butter would not be forgotten. The person assigned to get the butter didn't realize there were two packages and only grabbed half. We didn't discover the error until we got to camp—seven miles from a store. One of our favorite camping breakfasts was biscuits with jam and Dad often provided fresh trout to go with it. Mother came to me wondering what to do. Rather than blame the person who left the butter behind, she was trying to figure out how not to need it. Finally, she came up with the idea of strawberry crumpets. She dissolved Jell-O, added it to the biscuit mix, and loudly announced, "Everyone knows you don't use butter with strawberry crumpets." The crumpets were delicious and became a family tradition. To this day, no one uses butter on the strawberry crumpets.

If you are unable to attend the service for a close friend, send a written remembrance instead. Here is a story I wrote for a dear friend's memorial service. I'm including it because maybe someday one of you or someone you share it with will need to know about 'rolling over and digging in' (both literally and figuratively).

"I first met her when I was a youngster at church, but got to know her better while our families car-camped, back-packed, and took long trips together. I don't remember calling her anything but her nick-name. She was known so universally by her nick-name that she almost signed a will that way before remembering it wasn't on her birth certificate.

"In 1966, she took a six-week summer trip to Europe with Mom and Dad. Their trip began with two weeks of hiking the Alps. For safety, they were roped together whenever traversing significant snow. Once, she decided to follow the example of some other hikers and use her jacket as a sled to get to the trail below. It was great fun until she started going too fast and had trouble stopping. After stopping, she discovered the rest of the snow field she saw was on a different mountain. She had stopped near the edge of a cliff. She didn't dare climb back up to the trail until she again had a rope around her.

"At breakfast, shortly after returning to the states, Mom asked us what we would do if we found ourselves sliding on our back in the snow and couldn't stop. My brother answered that he would position himself so he could use his feet to stop. Mom shocked us by screaming, "No! You roll over and dig in with your teeth, your chin, your nose, your fingers, your hands, your elbows, your knees, and your toes." She pantomimed using them all to slow down, and she made a grotesque figure balanced on one leg.

"Just a week later, my brother and three companions were scaling a steep 13,000 foot pass in the Sierra Nevada Mountains with no trail. They chose to descend via a steep snow slope because it was more stable than the loose shale. My brother slipped. He rapidly picked up speed, sliding on the sleeping bag tied to the bottom of his heavy pack as he tried unsuccessfully to stop with his feet. He was praying he would be okay when the snow turned to granite below, when he heard Mom's, "No! You roll over and dig in." On his stomach, stopping was easy. He was able to warn the others to roll over and dig in just before the next person slipped. To this day, I'm not the only one grateful my friend was adventuresome enough to go sliding on her jacket in the Alps."

Summary
- Embrace opportunities for public speaking
- Listening allows you to learn from others
- Learn to consciously read body language
- Find your negotiation style and make it a strength
- Sharing through writing builds your reputation
- Present a professional appearance
- Pay attention to the social graces—remembering names, thank yous, condolences, and congratulations.

3

Getting Yourself Under Control

I once considered myself an organized person. I sailed through college balancing four to six heavy courses and my homework was always turned in. It wasn't until more than a decade into my career that I cried for help. My system worked as long as I only needed to plan for myself. I could do marathons as needed. However, as a manager I realized it wasn't fair to my team to allow things to drift into crisis mode. Not everyone enjoys doing the impossible on a deadline. I needed to do a better job setting goals and making long-term plans so the group had more time and could enjoy executing the plan.

The time management course I took helped me appreciate what poor work habits I had. I ran on intuition and it worked well much of the time. I multiplexed and responded to requests, but one day I realized I was *reacting* rather than *acting*. Someone else was setting the agenda and I was doing my best to fill in the pieces. If you want to control your life, you need to organize your life. Otherwise, you will spend your time reacting to the demands of others instead of taking charge.

Procrastination

Procrastination is not necessarily a bad thing. Fairly early in my career I told my manager I had to stop procrastinating. He didn't agree. He said I just didn't work linearly. Multitasking is a skill that allows you to juggle several projects simultaneously, and when properly developed, it can increase your productivity tremendously. There will always be times when your part of a project waits on someone else's part. You must be able to switch gears and work on something else while you wait. And you must be able to switch back immediately when the time comes for your next step. Reacting is an important as acting, but you don't want it to be your only skill.

I often started a project promptly and got the research done early. But when it came to writing, work expanded to fill the time allocated to it. Writer's block. I gave myself permission to play hooky.

Playing hooky is more fun when there is something waiting to be done. A few times a year I visited the public library and spent the day reading children's books. I went home and read a few more before heaving a contented sigh of satisfaction and going to sleep. These days correlated strongly with the next major crisis and weeks of long hours. I thrived on the long hours because I'd had my play time. These times also correlated with my need to make a conscious choice to change directions or to do something different. While I played, my unconscious mind dealt with my problem. Later, I was willing to make the necessary decision.

I worked with a colleague who had at least half the job done in half the time. He was likely to bring his projects in early. I admired this skill, and often felt guilty because it wasn't my mode of working. I thought I should be able to work in a more organized fashion.

Procrastination wasn't a new habit for me. For years, I had a bed on the porch. The porch was converted into an all-year bedroom by wrapping it in plastic for the winter. I loved sleeping on the porch. In summer, it got the first night breezes. We didn't have air-conditioning until years later, so that mattered. But the porch had one drawback. It was cold in winter. Fortunately, winters were usually above freezing and an electric blanket solved the problem for sleeping. However, first thing in the morning I jumped out of bed, grabbed my school clothes, and ran for the door to the main house. Needless to say, my bed was left unmade. The only time I returned would be to put something away or pick up something for school, and by then I was running late. Summer or winter, I consistently put off making my bed.

One day I came home from school and Mom took me out to the porch. She showed me my unmade bed and told me my sister's best-friend's mother came by while I was at school and when they went to the porch to get something out of storage, there was my messy bed. Mom said she told the woman, "Joan can't seem to remember to make her bed until she is ready to go to sleep. That is her problem." I was embarrassed. I was also cured, at least of that particular mode of procrastination.

I created a little story about the FBI coming into my room to look for something while I was out. I didn't want them to get the wrong impression, so I remembered to make my bed in the morning instead of waiting until bedtime. This worked all through college, graduate school, and work. Whenever I was tempted to do it later, I would think of those poor FBI agents who would have to look at my unmade bed. The bed got made, and my bedroom stopped being an embarrassment to Mom and me.

Sometimes we procrastinate because we assume a task will take more time than it really does. The book *Speed Cleaning* recommends timing various cleaning chores. The author claims we mentally exaggerate the effort a job takes, particularly one we want to avoid. I still remember the shock of discovering that vacuuming my living room was not a twenty-five minute job, but a seven minute job. If you allow things to linger on your 'dread list' because you think they will take too much time, investigate your assumptions. You may find out your two-hour bugaboo only takes fifteen minutes to perform.

Part of dealing with procrastination is understanding the reasons you procrastinate. Is it because the task holds no interest for you? If so, maybe you should look for the opportunity to pass the task along to someone else. Amazingly, some people actually enjoy the things I most dread.

If you procrastinate because your mind is subconsciously dealing with the problem and seeking a solution, perhaps you shouldn't attempt to cure your procrastination. In fact, you may not be procrastinating at all. 'Sleep on it' isn't just a delaying tactic. It is a well-known method of weighing variables and coming to a decision.

You can deal with procrastination in a variety of ways. Make up stories to motivate yourself. Make games out of chores you'd rather avoid. Time yourself, so you know what the real time-cost of a chore is. You may be spending more time avoiding the task than you would spend accomplishing it. Give yourself consequences (making up the bed before you get into it) for failure to complete chores.

There are some excellent books to help you stop procrastinating. Two titles I recommend are *Doing it Now* and *Getting Things Done* by E. Bliss. Both are light reads, but teach you ways to break up big projects into manageable pieces. A big project can be overwhelming. Several small projects just take a little bit of time each.

If procrastination is a problem for you, figure out why. Deal with it. Decide what 'done' is.

Personal Organization

When I took that one-day time management course in 1988, I was primarily thinking in terms of how I used my time and how to prioritize 'to do' items, but the instructor pointed out that office clutter is a great time waster. I determined to organize my office.

We've all seen those neat little signs, "A clean desk is a sign of a sick mind." I'm not a doctor of psychiatry, so I can't say if that's true. I can say with certainty that you cannot find things as quickly in a cluttered office as in a clean office. My sister-in-law demonstrated this when she nearly missed her flight to Mexico. The airline refused to issue a boarding pass when she presented her driver's license, her credit card, her ATM card, and her expired passport as identification. They required her birth certificate as well. Unworried, she returned home to pluck it from the cluttered desk. Although she rarely cleans, she claimed to know exactly where it would be. An hour later—without her birth certificate—she returned to the airport and arranged to sign a notarized document swearing she was born in Texas.

A clean office is not the result of a genetic trait; it requires conscious effort. According to that time management class, color is a useful reminder. I bought expensive colored Pendaflex folders. I worked at establishing a system for the colors. The only one I still use is yellow for invention disclosures and patent applications. Otherwise, I enjoy seeing a rainbow of colors every time I open my drawer, but the colors do help. You tend to remember the color of a particular folder, even if there is no systematic color coding. Once you develop a habit, such as filing, or putting things away, it makes your life easier. Instead of simply bragging that you can find what you need when you need it, you actually *can* find what you need.

Time management is more than organizing your files and cleaning your office. You will also learn to organize your contacts, maintain your appointment files, prioritize tasks, and decide what a project entails. If you have the opportunity to take a time management class, do so. You will learn something different from what I learned. Be sure to pass along what you learn to others in your network.

Decide when to start

Half of deciding what 'done' means, is deciding when to start. This used to be particularly hard for me because I tended to allow work to fill the available time. By delaying the start, I wasted less time. Make appointments with yourself. The first appointment is to get started. Use the appointment time to list the tasks involved and see if you need to get others involved. Use the time to determine if the task is worth doing.

Excellence vs. Perfection

Trying to make anything perfect is a waste of time and takes away from more important things like family life and helping others. Most of us know when something is good enough for its intended purpose. The perfectionist goes all out to make everything perfect, but in the process wastes a great deal of time and effort when perfection isn't necessary. I am a reformed perfectionist. Now I am content if something is 'good enough'. Remember my third-level manager's story about invention disclosures? If it works, if it does the job you want it to do (no matter what 'it' is) then it's probably good enough. Ask yourself if anything is gained by taking excellence to the next step and achieving perfection. Ask yourself if perfection is even possible.

Think about the highway system in your city. Is it perfect? Does traffic flow freely at all hours of the day or night? Of course not. Rush-hour creates traffic jams and back-ups all over the country. The highways are inadequate to handle the number of cars traveling on them. So what's the solution? Build more highways, of course. Expand existing highways to make them wider. But while you expand those highways, fewer cars can travel on them, due to lane-closures, and the time involved in the construction means traffic count increases so that by the time the expansion is completed, the roads are once again too small to carry the load. The perfect highway system can only be built in the absence of traffic, and in the absence of traffic, the perfect highway system is unnecessary.

Now consider whatever project you are currently working on. Is it possible to achieve perfection? How long will it take? How much money is required? Is it worth it? Instead of trying to create the perfect widget—which may well become obsolete before you go to market—create the best widget you can with the time and resources allocated. Last year I had to remind myself of this. I was tempted to proofread a conference paper one more time before its original submission. If it had been a submission to a journal, I'd have known the effort for perfection was unnecessary until reviewers' comments had been incorporated. I knew the paper was good enough. Finally, I recommended my co-author enjoy getting ready for her vacation rather than spending more time on the paper.

If you find yourself striving for perfection, instead of accepting excellence, you may need to reassess your priorities. Can you spend your time and energy more wisely?

Paper Audit Trails

Paper audits are a task engineers ignore to their detriment. A consultant once told me, "Most engineers don't understand the importance of leaving an auditable paper trail." My first manager warned me to beware of a particular manager. That individual had a way of scoffing at a new idea and then inventing it himself six months later. My manager knew the importance of having the other man witness his lab book. Then when the other manager re-invented the invention, there was no controversy. The man's signature effectively meant he gave up any rights to the invention when he thought it was a poor idea. He couldn't make claims on it later.

Good records are essential for a patent defense. If you claim to have invented something, you need to show it didn't already exist. You must show due diligence. And you need to be able to show when you began working on it. Having a colleague witness the original invention in an engineering notebook makes defense much easier than having no records.

A friend of mine kept reasonable records, but one of his patents was contested many years after the original experiments. His lab book notations had not been witnessed for the first successful working experiment. That successful working experiment established a critical inventorship date. Fortunately, his lab technician (when that breed still existed) observed the test and vividly remembered the results. The lab technician was still around and gave a legal deposition. The lawsuit was dropped immediately upon the plaintiff's lawyers seeing the records, including the deposition.

An auditable paper trail also means a cover-up is more difficult if not impossible. Pressuring an engineer to perjure himself is unlikely to succeed (or even be attempted) if there are too many records to destroy.

A couple of years into our participation on the JPEG committee, I learned of a letter claiming the facsimile data compression standard violated three patents. These patents were expired, but lawsuits can go back five years to cover the time when they were still valid. A law firm had found patents in other fields and claimed they applied to the fax data compression technique. I still had copies of papers from when I entered the field, and found plenty of examples of prior art in my files, which I could provide to a US fax standards committee participant. Having supplied the necessary information, I heard nothing more about the problem.

The experience convinced me to save every JPEG document in an organized manner. I ended up with over fifteen linear feet of binders. I knew the importance of keeping an auditable paper trail. With the fax standard, I had saved only the gory technical contributions. It never occurred to me the rest might be needed.

Avoid memo wars

Never carry out a battle in writing. One of my first employees was a 'manager trainer'. He described a situation where two people disagreed and exchanged memos on the subject. Each posted the memo from his opponent above his computer terminal. The memo was a constant irritant and when the individual became thoroughly angry, they responded. (After all, why respond calmly and reasonably if you can wait until you're fighting mad?) The argument escalated into outright warfare. My employee recommended not putting personal disagreements in writing. He said it was much better to deal with disagreements in person and then forget about them and let them go. That way, instead of ongoing warfare you can at least reach détente.

I once had someone I had considered a good working colleague and personal friend threaten to take my co-inventor and me to an ethics board. He claimed he had personally invented a key idea in our patent, and had shared his earlier system with me. Because I knew the details of his system, he assumed my co-inventor (who worked on that piece) had known about it too. He sent me his PASCAL program (which I didn't know how to read) and claimed it as proof. My manager tried to arbitrate the conflict. It dragged on for more than a year.

The problem threatened to raise its ugly head again after I had transferred to a new position, so I felt I needed to alert my new manager. In the process of letting him know what had happened, I showed my new manager the ½ inch-thick file of the other man's documentation. Our accuser had saved notes on every phone conversation, memo, chat in the hallway, or other interaction we'd ever had. My co-inventor and I only had a few items to demonstrate the work had evolved independently, including an e-mail from my accuser that contradicted his position and was not included in his file. My new manager said he had learned to beware of either too much documentation or no documentation at all. The problem disappeared.

Good researchers keep good records, but are too busy doing research to be packrats. Record your inventions. Have your lab book witnessed. Maintain proper documentation. Be prepared to provide proof of inventorship.

Don't keep every scrap of paper anyone ever sends you—particularly if it makes you mad. Memo wars are a waste of time and energy. Don't act unless you are quiet and at peace inside. If you find yourself driving to work rehearsing a big drama with you as the central character, don't take action. The drama, thunder, lightning, and crashing cymbals are emotionalism. Don't give them power over your life.

Clutter Control

According to that time management class, clutter is a great time-waster. If you don't believe that, time yourself the next time you have to lay hands on something. My sister-in-law spent an hour looking for her birth certificate, and didn't find it. If you are one of those naturally organized and tidy people, you may want to skip to the last page of this chapter. For those of you who suffer from clutter, read on.

After taking the time management class, I organized my office, but I still lived in clutter at home. I was in the habit of allowing unread magazines to stack up and create huge piles. My kitchen counter kept accumulating items unrelated to the kitchen. According to my December 30, 1990 diary, "I made a goal to establish a habit of tidiness in my life. I am tired of living in clutter. I can see that if I knew where to put things the clutter would be unnecessary. Since I expect occasional appointments to look at books, my house needs to stay clean and tidy. It will also help make it possible to work and run a home business." Resolutions are good things. Even better if you can put them into practice.

Everything needs a home

Most clutter results from failing to decide where an item belongs. I am consistent about putting away items that have homes. File folders go in file drawers, tools go in the tool box, and socks go in the sock drawer. That part is easy. But if you don't have a tool box, your new hammer is likely to go on the kitchen table or cabinet. You have to decide where to put things. Once you've given an item a home, keeping clutter under control becomes easier.

De-cluttering became a multiple year process. I wrote on May 27, 1991, "This morning I finally tackled some of the clutter. I like the wood-grained magazine storage boxes and I sorted the large pile of magazines from my dining room into some of the boxes. I need to decide if I want to collect magazines, and if so, where to store them. Perhaps I would be better off selling them or shipping them off to developing countries." At least I was beginning to think about getting rid of some of the clutter.

My sister directed me to the hilarious book, *The Side-Tracked Home Executives*. I carefully read the book and tried to implement the authors' system for making sure household tasks were done. Unfortunately, I could never remember to check my 'to do' each day. The system didn't work for me.

Late in 1994, I read *Clutter's Last Stand* and *How to Get Organized When You Don't Have the Time*. I found *Clutter's Last Stand* more motivational. It actually helped me understand why 'dejunking' is desirable. The other book gave specific ideas that worked for me. Both books taught me to ask the question, "Would someone else be able to use this?" As a result, I donated my old computer to my sister's school. If you don't need it, get rid of it.

When I moved, in the summer of 1994, I took several days to systematically open and discard junk mail. The junk mail problem disappeared when I realized it was repetitious. Friends tell me they open their junk mail over the outside garbage can. They don't even carry it into the house. Junk mail is just that—junk. If you need your carpets cleaned, you will receive another offer next week. Don't save the coupon from last week.

My local library has a magazine give-away table. The librarians are thrilled to receive used magazines since so many people pick them up. Spend a few minutes looking to see if the magazine has an article of interest to you. If so, rip it out and tear the top corner of the cover to indicate the magazine is not intact. About once a month, take your magazines to the library.

When the urge to de-clutter comes upon you, take advantage of it. That way it won't be such an onerous task, and while you putter about clearing away the mess, your mind has the opportunity to work on other things. When I started this book, some of the time I had set aside for working on the book proposal went to de-cluttering.

While you go through your accumulation of clutter, sort it carefully. Some of what you have failed to put away may have value. The paperwork from the purchase of your home—the ones you laid on the coffee table six or eight months ago—need a home. The health insurance package from your new employer needs a home. The carpet cleaning coupon throws away, along with the six new ones you've received in the past six months.

I have found a connection between the state of clutter in my home and the indecisiveness in my thinking. Some people garden and discard weeds. I de-clutter and discard junk. I suspect the feeling I get from clearing the surface of a table is similar to the feeling a gardener gets looking at a weed-free yard.

One of the books I read encouraged a gradual withdrawal from clutter rather than a dramatic one-step transformation. I found withdrawal worked well for me. Instead of kicking myself because the table is littered again, I vow to clear off half the table. This involves sorting through the junk and finding permanent places for about half the items—a job generally doable in an hour or so. Then I refuse to allow new junk in the cleared space. I can only place junk on the messy part of the table. The next time I clean, I increase the cleared space by about 50%, so the table is only one quarter cluttered. Soon everything has a place. If an item has a place, put it away. If it doesn't have a place, either find one or decide it doesn't need a place and get rid of it.

Do not allow unread periodicals to pile up. They become a fire hazard, as well as making your personal space less inviting. Try the magazine trick. You aren't planning to read everything in the magazine, so why save it? Save the article instead.

Articles make great airport and plane reading. As you read them, lighten your load. If you travel much, you will find this trick helps keep you current in your field. You'll also find if you are concentrating on an article instead of a light novel, your seatmates don't talk to you, so if you enjoy talking to people on airplanes, save the articles for other times.

Do you need it?

There are effective ways to control clutter. A friend of a friend claims that for every item that comes into her house, an equivalent item must leave—usually headed for the rubbish pile. This was her husband's rule, and it effectively controlled clutter.

Dad's rule was, "If you haven't used it in a year, sell it, give it away, or throw it out." He did exclude some wedding gifts and kitchen utensils from the rule, and sometimes I heard two years instead of one, but you get the idea. If you are storing something you don't use, stop storing it. There may be someone who needs it, and you obviously don't.

One of the things I find works well is to pack unused items into unmarked boxes and then store them in the basement for six months. At the end of six months if I haven't missed the items, it is easy to load them into the car and drive them to the drop off point for a nonprofit organization. You can also downsize as you move between houses, packing some boxes labeled only for storage at the destination. After six months if you have not missed anything, call a nonprofit and have them clear out the storage. In any case, the key is never to look inside the boxes. If you can't remember what was in the box, and you haven't missed anything, you no longer need whatever you stored. I remember the agony of cleaning out 15 years of 'saved items' once, and it was once too often.

One way to think about your home is to calculate a value per square foot, and then decide if your treasures are worth the value of the space they take. Ask yourself, "Are the stored items worth that much?" In many cases, the answer is "No" and that makes giving things away easier. Once you have cleaned out all those stored treasures, the space is freed up for active living. This process is even easier if you have rented a storage unit. Clean it out and you can free up a few extra dollars every month.

You can get rid of a tremendous amount of clutter by having a garage sale. In 1994, I downsized from a four bedroom house in New York to a two bedroom apartment in southern Vermont. I had the firm assistance of my sister-in-law in deciding what to keep and what to get rid of. She organized a weekend garage sale. My garage floor started out covered with stuff, except for narrow walkways. When the sale ended there was barely enough stuff to cover those walkways. Things flew out of the garage so fast I didn't have time to grieve over their passing. Sell what you don't need.

When my sister-in-law helped me buy furniture in Colorado, we furnished four rooms from scratch in six days. The total cost was less than nine years of storage payments plus the cost of moving my old furniture from Vermont to Colorado and a lot less hassle.

Some things are worth keeping, even if it costs you time and money to keep them. My new dining room table is beautiful. It has a light hickory top and cherry legs. I found a woodworker who co-designed the perfect buffet to match it. The top and bottom are hickory supported by cherry legs. The sides and shelves are glass so you can see all of my mementos. This set I will take with me if I ever move again. It's worth paying to move it.

If your home or office is so disorganized you can't stand it, set up files. Clean off your desk. Put things away. Sell, give away, or throw away things you don't use or no longer love. Keep what's important. You don't have to put *everything* away, just everything you aren't using. It's easier to organize your thinking when your space is organized.

House Cleaning

Despite the progress we have made in the past few decades, housekeeping is still a woman's job. When people visit your home, they look at the condition of the house. If it is clean and neat, they form an opinion of the woman who lives there. They think of her as well-organized and virtuous. If the house is messy, dirty, or cluttered, they think of her as disorganized, with sloppy personal habits. This is generally true whether the man or the woman of the house has taken responsibility for cleaning. And it is a fact; other people's perceptions of us affect us.

Men have a distinct advantage over women in the area of housekeeping. A single man is not expected to maintain a clean house. Men can be sloppy. Women cannot.

This expectation affects our work-life as well as our home-life. Those of us who are not dedicated to keeping a clean house suffer from guilt. The guilt nags at us when we get up in the morning, when we come home in the evening, and particularly when we expect (fear, perhaps) guests to drop in. The guilt we carry with us distracts us from our work and limits our community involvement. There are almost always tasks left undone at home.

When I bought a four bedroom house, cleaning became a chore I avoided, except the kitchen and bathroom. I dreaded the job so much I just kept putting it off. Finally, I'd waste an entire Saturday and get the job done, but I didn't enjoy it.

Unless you must trade a cleaning service for such basics as food and rent, invest in the cleaning service. Eating out less often will pay for periodic cleaning. Consider how much time you spend on cleaning and appreciate the service provided by someone else. Add the time your spouse spends and the time you spend nagging about it. Multiply those hours by *your* hourly wage. The table below can give you a starting point. I calculated by assuming fifty weeks per year, forty hours per week to make the numbers come out nice. This is what you are currently 'paying' for housecleaning.

Once you find your cleaning person, do not accept a 'bargain,' and pay in cash. Your person may not pay Social Security and they will regret it when retirement time rolls around. You may regret it as well if you are ever subject to the kind of personal investigation public figures are regularly involved in. How would it be if you lost the nomination for Vice President because you paid your cleaning lady under the table? Rates vary by area, but twenty dollars an hour is not unreasonable for a good cleaning person.

Table 1. Hourly rates

Annual salary	Hourly Wage	Comments Hourly Wage multiplied by 50 weeks @ 40 hours per week
$10,000	$5.00	Not enough to live on.
$20,000	$10.00	Could you live on this?
$40,000	$20.00	This is reasonable.
$60,000	$30.00	You may need to pay this in affluent communities.
$80,000	$40.00	You should be able to find someone for less.

If your person cleans multiple homes, they are an independent contractor and are responsible for their own Social Security. Don't encourage them to save the 16% (8% employee contribution and 8% the employer normally pays) by not paying into the system. Make sure you factor Social Security into your payment. You need to complete and file a 1099 form for your housekeeper.

A clean house takes longer to get dirty. I suspect the dust and dirt doesn't move from room to room, but actually leaves the house. Between major cleanings, light cleaning—including an occasional vacuuming—keeps everything ready for guests. The benefits of a cleaning service go beyond the time not spent cleaning. You also save the time spent avoiding the work and the guilt that interferes in your life and prevents you from doing things that are more enjoyable.

Share tasks with a friend

Window washing requires the right kind of tools, and many cleaning services don't do windows. My sister recommends a dish cloth covered with nylon mesh for scrubbing off stuck on junk, then a squeegee to remove most of the water, followed by paper towels to wipe off the Windex. I tried this, and it worked.

My sister also joins forces with a friend when faced with this task. The two of them wash the windows at both their houses. Two people can wash windows at least three times faster than one, so even doing the windows on two houses is faster than working alone on one.

Of course, many people, men as well as women, use house cleaning time to increase their productivity. While your conscious mind is occupied with vacuuming, mopping, and scrubbing, your unconscious mind is free to work on real problems. After all, it doesn't take much thought to scrub a toilet. You may find solutions to work-related problems pop into your head while your hands busy themselves with brushes and cleanser.

If cleaning house isn't a relaxing change of pace for you, hire someone else to do it. There is nothing inherently moral about scrubbing floors. Look at your hourly wage again. Would you pay someone else that amount of money to run the vacuum?

Pairing up at work

Pairing up at work can speed up unpleasant tasks as well. I often volunteer to do a task I enjoy, like composing the first draft of a progress report, if the other person will do a first draft of a drawing. It usually takes us each about the same time, but both jobs are done much faster than if either of us had done both chores. Choose the task you enjoy and do well and neither of you is stuck with an onerous burden.

It still amazes me how some people enjoy jobs I despise. For example, it always seemed a poor trade-off to cook for two hours and then watch the family consume dinner in half an hour. On the other hand, the dishes could be hand-washed with a good table-clearer and a fast dryer in about the same half-hour. To this day, I'd rather clean up than cook. On the other hand, my youngest sister bakes cookies as therapy.

I still chuckle over a story I heard from some newlyweds. The husband manfully emptied the dishwasher after his wife had loaded and run it. It was several days before they discovered they had each volunteered for the task they despised. The husband considered it a challenge to pack as many dirty dishes into the dishwasher as possible, and he had a definite talent for packing it full. His wife hated dealing with the dirty dishes. The wife enjoyed handling the clean dishes and putting them carefully into their proper places. Her husband found unloading and putting away dishes boring. Once they learned one another's likes and dislikes they promptly switched jobs. I wonder how often similar things happen at work.

Use your time and energy efficiently. Maybe you won't always be able to pick and choose your favorite tasks and leave the onerous ones to someone else, but if you communicate with your colleagues, you may find you can offload more of the bad stuff than you think.

Summary

- Value your time; spend it wisely
- Getting organized saves you time
- Manage your procrastination; make appointments with yourself
- Strive for excellence, not perfection
- Leave paper audit trails
- De-clutter as needed
- Be willing to pay someone else to handle chores you don't enjoy

Part Two

The Next Steps

4

Managing Your Career

$\mathcal{M}$anaging your own career is a management opportunity available to everyone. An essential skill in that process is 'managing your manager'. Making it easy for your manager to do exactly what you want requires good communication and a willingness to take the initiative. Having multiple up-to-date resumes makes it easier for others to nominate you for awards, promotions, and career opportunities. One way to grow professionally—independently of what is happening in your company—is to join and work as a volunteer in 'your' professional organization. And of course, choosing projects in which you can shine makes a huge difference.

A key element in managing your career is understanding your company culture. Much of company culture can be learned simply from observing what happens around you—how others interact. More detailed information may be available from books written about your company or by company executives. Lou Gerstner's book, *Who Says Elephants Can't Dance?* is an excellent example. I found his observations to be much more accurate than many of the other books I have read about my company. Read what others have written about your company, and then check the facts against your own observations. And then check your observations with your mentors. Understanding your company culture can make—or break—your career.

You should also be aware that company culture may differ among divisions, departments, and even teams. Be observant at all times if you want to avoid mistakes.

Downsizing can happen

Sharkproof by Harvey Mackay is all about how to "get the job you want, keep the job you love..." It includes excellent advice on what to do while you are employed so you don't go into shock if you are downsized. I loved his chapter "You Can Own Your Own Business and Still Get Fired." The bank abruptly refused to loan him money he needed in order to stay in business. Statistics indicate 80% of Americans are fired at least once during their careers. I reached Mackay's conclusion that downsizing has nothing to do with individuals several years after he did. I wish I had read the book when it came out in 1993, and I encourage you to read it now. After you read it, encourage your college-aged children to read it as well. Years from now, the stories will come back to them when they need advice. The book may help them not to give up when times get tough. More importantly, it will start them off right and help them to understand why you need to join a professional organization, do volunteer work, learn all you can about your business, and network, network, network.

You are the CEO of your career

Jim Collins' book *Good to Great* talks about how 'good' companies can become 'great' companies. After you have read it once, I recommend you read it again while considering yourself the CEO of your own career. You need to learn to 'think like an owner'. Collins presents three questions: 1) What are you deeply passionate about?, 2) What can you be the best in the world at?, and 3) What drives your economic engine? As you consider those questions, think about yourself. And as you read about companies that failed to sustain growth, compare them to yourself. Are you facing challenges and growing from them, or do you accept defeat readily?

I particularly liked the section under the heading "Start a 'Stop Doing' List." Doing more and more is not a path to greatness. Instead, be disciplined about what you can be best in the world at and cut out most of the clutter that distracts you from achieving that goal. This concept will help you reach your goals. A 'Stop Doing List' can be a significant step towards life/work balance. Expand the 20% of what you are doing which has 80% of the impact and cut in half the 80% of what you are doing which has only 20% of the impact. Then use some of the newly freed up time to think.

Chapter 4 "Confront The Brutal Facts (Yet Never Lose Faith)", describes different reactions to a new adversary. Collins' winners viewed competing with a new company as a challenge they could win since they could be best at what they had chosen to do. His losers (tops in their specific market) resigned themselves to being second best without putting up a fight. As described by Collins, "In confronting the brutal facts, the good-to-great companies left themselves stronger and more resilient, not weaker and more dispirited." I am reminded of a saying I once read, "You may not be able to control what happens to you, but you can always control what you think about (and how you react to) what happens to you." If you accept defeat, you have already failed.

Know the job descriptions for your career path

This is one of those 'do as I say, not as I did (early in my career)' lessons.

If you don't know where you want to go, it's difficult to plan a path to take you there. More than a decade into my career, I saw a summary of the engineering and programming levels. I was shocked. At Research, there were no obvious levels. I started as a Research Staff Member and could have continued my entire career with that job description. In fact, the only open transition was to Fellow. But when I read that summary, I realized that at each level, the employee was expected to have assumed more responsibilities. For example, you could attend a conference, present a paper at a conference, organize a session at a conference, or organize the conference.

These four roles follow the apprenticeship, independent worker, manager, and executive states. Another sequence is to read a paper, write a paper, write a book chapter, and write a book. This was when I realized every Fellow I knew had written a book. I later learned most Fellows in Research wrote books, but books are less common in the development divisions.

One way to check out your dream job is to ask to shadow someone in that job. Everyone is different, but watching the daily responsibility tells you a lot about the skills you will need to cultivate to enjoy the job. You may discover you don't want the job after all. I once shadowed an executive for a week. The person did an excellent job, but his day was so chopped up I didn't know how he managed to accomplish anything. By the end of the week, I didn't want to be an executive.

Know your strengths and what makes you happy

My strength lies in spontaneity. I may head off for a drink of water and not reappear for several hours. I'll meet a programmer in the halls. He mentions a major headache he's encountering on his project. We go to his office and use the white board to help me understand his problem. Before I leave his office, we'll have the kernel to a radical breakthrough. Together, we know we can solve the problem in an elegant way. This kind of spontaneous interaction has resulted in more inventions than I can list.

If you work best on the fly, it is important that you don't over-schedule yourself. You won't have time to be spontaneous.

If you work best in a structured environment, make the effort to assure yourself of that environment. Set times when others may interrupt your work and times when they must leave you alone to concentrate. One of my colleagues found this an easy solution to my constant interruptions. He worked best when allowed to concentrate, and interruptions dragged him out of working mode. Every minor interruption cost him time because he then had to work himself back into his 'zone'. Nobody else knows how interruptions affect your work, but you do. Explain, and be firm in your explanations. Give yourself the best possible working conditions.

Do you have an up-to-date resume?

If you need an introduction to someone, it helps to have an up-to-date resume. The introducer can forward your resume to the person you need to meet. That person quickly gains an appreciation of your background. For casual things like a request to shadow someone, the short version does quite well. Traditional wisdom recommends your resumes be one to two pages or two to four pages. A friend once told me the two to four page resume becomes appropriate after you have worked at least ten years. Usually, your resume should be tailored to the occasion.

Current resumes are useful for more than just job-hunting. My first job hunt took place while I was finishing my PhD. Back in the dark ages, secretaries did the typing. My resume was produced by the placement center and I only had hardcopy. In my first five years on the job, it never occurred to me to update my resume. After all, back then a position with IBM was a job for life. One day my manager's manager asked for my resume. I told him I only had the one left over from my job search. His response was, "I want to nominate you for White House Fellow. You have an hour to get me your up-to-date resume."

Equally important is what I call your long resume. This is an accumulation of everything. It explicitly cites every paper, every conference attended, and every patent. It provides the raw data for someone filling out a nomination form. The National Academy of Engineering nomination form, under "contribution record," asks for complete citations including all authors for five publications of "most significant impact." Then it has "Summary: refereed journal articles: __ patents: __ books: __ book chapters: __ proceedings: __ publications: __ other contributions of record: __." Your long resume, or another version without the publications, should have every job you ever worked at, every company address, and every manager's name.

You should already be collecting the information needed for a security clearance. I filled out the form as part of the process of job searching, and the questions went on for many pages. Have you ever tried to remember every address you ever lived at from age fifteen on? What about every trip outside the country, including the dates you entered and left each foreign country visited? A friend of mine used his old passports, but not all the stamps were readable. It took him over a month to reconstruct his life. It helps to collect this information while your parents and siblings are around to refresh your memory. More and more professionals will apply for security clearances, so get started early. It's better to have information you don't need than to need information you don't have.

Manage yourself

I used to catch myself thinking, "I can't be happy until X happens," or, "If only X would change, then I'd be happy." You can fill in X with an event, spouse, job, location, children, finances, economy, or just about anything else. Sometimes X is your manager. Instead of blaming outside circumstances people or events, learn to view obstacles as an opportunity to grow. It's easier to change yourself than X. I learned the hard way not to hand any person, place, thing, or event the power to make me unhappy.

If you think a person, event, or thing has the power to make you happy you will be disappointed. And if you are not happy, you will be tempted to blame the person, event, or thing for your unhappiness. Mom used to tell me marriage should be between two strong individuals, each of them well anchored, like a tree. Only the branches should intertwine. If one individual leans on another for their happiness or support, then when strong winds (troubles) come, both will crash. If only their branches intertwine, both are stronger. This rule is not limited to marriage. If you depend upon your job to make you happy, you will be devastated when your company goes through a cycle of downsizing. If you find your happiness in things—a car, a house, or anything else—you leave yourself open to misery if the thing is damaged or lost. Happiness must come from within or it cannot withstand exterior forces.

We often hear 'get revenge', 'get angry', or 'get mad'. I prefer my sister's advice to her new assistant. My sister, a lawyer for another company, was in the middle of tense negotiations. She took her assistant aside and explained, "We don't get angry, we don't get mad, we don't get revenge, we just outlast them." This advice works well in standards meetings and other critical settings. People who are in it for the glory don't really care about the result. They grow impatient with the long haul and eventually move on. It is easy to stay calm and reasonable, when you know you can 'just outlast them'.

When you find yourself frustrated or unhappy, look for the causes, and at the same time, look for the solutions. Write down the qualities of your ideal job. Then write down the qualities of the job you have. This makes it easy to see the differences between what you want and what you have. You may find what you have is closer to what you want than you thought. Next, figure out how you have to change. Remember, you can't change your manager, you can't change the people you work with, and you can't change the nature of the project. So what has to change in order for you to be happy? It may be something as simple as interacting more with others. That was the key to my attitude change. Or it may be interacting less with others—as happened when my colleague insisted I stop interrupting him. If you find such a huge disparity between your ideal job and your current job that you can't bring them into alignment, you know it's time to move on. That is also a solution.

Don't allow someone else to manipulate your success. During my first two years with IBM, I worked on a new ribbon technology that eventually led to the Quietwriter, a member of the Selectric typewriter line without a ball. My manager's manager thought it was helpful to stir up new researchers, so he tried to convince me that unless I *claimed* ninety-five percent of the credit on the joint project, I *deserved* only five percent of the credit. "Besides," he would say, "the project is never going to work." I allowed these brief interactions to give me internal conflict. I didn't want ninety-five percent of the credit, but five percent wasn't fair either. I opted out when the project was transferred to a group with ribbon-making expertise, but my manager stayed with the project another five years and went to the corporate recognition event to accept a big check. That was the last time I let someone else override my judgment without a fight. I knew the project was a winner from day one.

Managing your Manager

An employee's manager is expected to help them with their career. However, the manager has other duties, such as the responsibility to deliver projects on time and within budget. The manager often has little time to train an employee for future growth. It is the employee's responsibility to find an avenue for growth and not sit back waiting for the manager to make the first move. This empowers the employee to find opportunities and present his manager with good options when management approval is required. Often, the employee can sign up for a task or training opportunity and inform his manager of his new skills when they have been mastered.

Because your manager has other duties, you need to make it easy for him or her to do what you want them to do. Years ago, I had an employee who was overdue for a promotion. I had never promoted anyone, so I kept avoiding the task. Around closing time one Friday evening, just before I left for vacation, an envelope slid under my door. The envelope contained a handwritten letter. My employee wrote, "It was not clear to me that you understood everything I have done this year so I'm listing them in this note to you." It went on for several pages. That night I prepared his promotion letter and sent it off to my manager to start the process. His promotion sailed through. Without that letter under my door, who knows when I would have acted? My employee knew how to manage me.

Some people think a promotion is an official anointing that will magically cause them to make the mental transition to the next level and cause others to offer them tasks at that level. They keep looking for someone, presumably their manager, to give them opportunities to shine so they can prove they are ready for the new job. That's not how it works. Instead, the engineer or programmer takes on additional responsibilities as they grow. Eventually they outgrow their old job and have taken on the duties and responsibilities of the new position. At

IBM, you get promotions after you are working at the next level.

The difference between career success and failure is often just not quitting. However, I will kill my own projects if I decide it is advisable. Once I've concluded something I'm working on is no longer a top priority, I consult with the others on the project. Usually, we have all recognized something more important has come along. Then I consult with my manager. If you choose to do this, mention the more important opportunity first, and get your manager enthused about the possibilities. Then put your thoughts into writing and copy both the workers and the managers. Lead with the new priority so the reasons you want to stop work on the old project are clear. This way you make it easy for your manager to do what you want.

Your manager can't help you if you don't let him know there's a problem. When the ribbon project wound down, I returned to ultrasonic printing. Unfortunately, I thought I had to listen to upper management, and they wanted to take the technology in a direction I knew was doomed to failure. I never told them it wouldn't work. After nine months, I told my manager I thought the project was stupid. So did he. We agreed the project would get back on its original track, and we already had proof it would work.

I waited nine months before talking to my manager about my dissatisfaction. Why did I wait so long? The answer is simple, I cry. Just thinking about having to admit I've failed makes my throat seize up. The more I fight to control my reaction, the more uncontrollable it becomes. My throat gets tight. The tears start to prickle at the back of my eyes and the fear that I'm going to humiliate myself by crying just compounds the problem.

Talking the problem over with other women, I've found it's very common. When we have to admit to failure or challenge authority, the reaction comes over us unbidden and we can't stop the process. Even reviewing things later can bring on another bout of tears. My sister-in-law tells about fighting tears on the way to the principal's office, only to arrive and learn she was the first National Merit Scholar ever from her school. Being called to the principal's office meant bad news. Admitting failure to your manager is bad news.

Uncontrollable tears are nothing more than stress demanding a way out. If you ignore them, they pass. In most cases, you aren't actually upset—you're just reacting on the outside. If tears are a problem for you, face the problem and ask for a box of tissues. Don't make the problem worse by waiting too long to address your issues.

Don't introduce the problem if you don't have a solution

Before taking the Advanced Management class, I thought executives were paid the big bucks to make the hard decisions, so I assumed my job would be to collect information and present the alternatives. I was wrong. Executives are paid the big bucks to prevent us from making costly mistakes. The employee's job is to collect the information, organize the alternatives, and after briefly presenting the alternatives with pros and cons, make a recommendation and have the implementation letter ready for signature. Some managers may want to reach independent conclusions, but most want all the information and the proper conclusion presented to them.

Some management models, particularly strongly hierarchical models, consider the act of making your manager 'look bad' as insubordination. Going to your manager with an unsolved problem and dumping it in his lap is not being a 'team player'. You can present a problem as long as you can also recommend a solution. Always come prepared. It's also a good idea to run your possible solution by some of the senior technical people. Perhaps they will prefer to bring the problem and solution forward, or they may know something that makes your recommendation unfeasible.

Never supply the problem

I had a manager who started to yell at me about once a year, after many years of encouragement. He accused me of 'doing it again'. The longer he talked the madder he got and eventually he lost his temper. I had no idea what 'it' was, but I always felt so guilty, I'd apologize madly and rush to end the interview.

In *The Gentle Art of Verbal Self-Defense*, Susan Elgin shows examples of verbal abuse where the victim supplies the problem. One of the defenses is to insist on an example and not accept that a problem exists until you understand it. After reading the book, I asked for an example. Since he couldn't give me one, he stopped yelling at me. However, our détente didn't solve the underlying problem.

About a year later, three executives whom I barely knew each asked me to demonstrate some technology. Each time, I explained one of my employees had done the work and I'd gladly arrange for him to give the demo. I never heard from them again. I wondered if someone was checking off 'mentor and encourage female managers' for their evaluation, so I told my manager. That was the 'it'. Making sure the people who did the work got the credit for the work was one of his hot buttons. He could not understand, "How, or even why, I was hogging the credit." He was shocked to learn I had confessed and apologized without having any idea of my crime.

Don't apologize for something until you know what 'it' is and you know you were guilty. Saying you're sorry and you'll never do 'it' again just makes the problem worse. My sister-in-law shared an example of mismanaging your manager, and mismanaging your career. At the same time, her example demonstrates managerial incompetence. Try not to be guilty of either.

Late one evening, her manager called her into his office and opened the conversation with, "You didn't lease enough space. All of your work has to be done over." *Never blame the employee for doing what you told them to do.* She went into defensive mode. "I leased exactly what the client asked for," and continued, giving the client's rationale for their requirements. As an employee or contractor, *never blame the client.* Placing blame is counter-productive. It does not solve the problem. It only creates bad feelings on all sides.

The manager dismissed the facts as irrelevant (which they were) and went on to explain that the engineering firm had spent weeks attempting to design a site within the leasehold. He had spent hours doing the same thing. "It's impossible."

He demonstrated by placing scaled paper cut-outs of building and pole within an area marked off on graph paper. Sure enough, the 'pole' extended over the fence line. Without thinking, my sister-in-law leaned across the desk and pushed the 'pole' to the side of the 'building', instead of at the end where the manager had placed it. "Buildings are ported on the sides as well as the ends. You still have room for the parking space inside the fence." Then she noticed the look on her manager's face.

Never make your manager look foolish. You manager can promote you, or he can make your life miserable. Don't go out of your way to give him reason to make you unhappy. If she had controlled her reactions, she could have offered to study the problem overnight and presented the solution the next day. Instead, she acted before thinking, and turned his several hours of figuring and fiddling into an exercise in stupidity. And of course, he made her life miserable.

Networking

It is important to make connections, both socially and professionally. More and more people telecommute at least part time these days. This cuts down on the interaction so necessary for personal and career growth. Fortunately, we can work within our professional societies and meet real people with common interests. Your company will treat you better if they know you are known outside. Connections outside the workplace give you more freedom inside. It is hard to trap someone who knows they can get a job instantly somewhere else. Networking is one of the recurring topics in this book. You must begin, this very day, to build your support network. Your career depends upon it.

Through the years, I've worked out a system for keeping information about people I meet at conferences and meetings. I write on the front of the other person's card, the context in which I met them, including the date. On the back, I write what I have promised to do for them, such as send them a particular reprint. If I want the other person to do something for me, I write it on the back of my card and give it to them. If your company refuses to supply you with business cards, make your own. They are essential. You define yourself as nonprofessional when you don't have cards.

At my first standards meeting, individuals met newcomers and exchanged business cards during the breaks. I didn't have cards. The head of my company delegation gave me some of his cards and had me write my information on the back. Don't let this happen to you.

Benefits of joining a professional society

You must have affiliations on your resume. To fail to belong to a professional organization is to identify yourself as not being a professional. I've frequently told mentees, "Don't come back until you have picked a professional organization and joined it." Joining and participating in your professional organization is part of giving back to your profession. I'm amazed at the number of engineers and programmers who drop their membership because of the cost per year. They ask, "What is it doing for me?" and conclude, "Not much." This always reminds me of John F. Kennedy's quote, "Ask not what your country can do for you, but ask what you can do for your country." Someone before you worked to make your profession recognized as a respected *profession* and not just any old job. You need to continue the effort for the next generation.

You need to make a difference in your chosen professional society. Don't just join—join in the work. Increase your outside visibility by participating in the planning of conferences. Increase your visibility by submitting papers and speaking at conferences. Increase your visibility and demonstrate leadership through your society activities. Increase your visibility by nominating others for the honors your society bestows.

The magazines published by your chosen organization will allow you to stay current in your field. Read the articles pertaining to your field, and at least some of the articles pertaining to related fields. Television commercials are a great time to browse through technical magazines. Rip out the interesting articles and save them for later reading and potential filing.

Having your papers published in a refereed journal counts more than in a conference proceedings or an un-refereed magazine. 'Refereed journals' are usually supported by professional societies. IBM's Research and Development Journal is also a refereed journal. Often, the better papers (or a longer version) from a conference are requested as submissions for a journal. If you receive such a request, follow through. These are the publications that can contribute to your external reputation and help you progress in your career.

Head hunters

About every six months I hear from a head hunter. If they are looking for certain skills, I'm willing to listen and give their name to someone who is out of work. You can increase your network significantly by being willing to refer your friends, colleagues, and associates for other positions. They may not be interested, but they will appreciate being thought of and respected enough to be recommended. Never pass along a resume without permission.

If you are actually looking for work, beware of head hunters who are not on retainer. A retainer means a company has hired the head hunter to find the right person for them. The head hunter is paid even if no one is hired. Head hunters on commission are more interested in collecting resumes and getting them to companies. Once they send out your resume, if you are hired within a year (no matter how) they get their commission. They may not look for a good skill match, so the first question you ask is, "Are you on retainer?" Beware of anything but a straightforward, "Yes." If not on retainer, they may forward your resume to multiple companies and once a company receives your resume from them, the head hunter can demand payment if you are hired. This makes you more expensive for the hiring company, and may make your job search harder.

Make friends

Network outside your field of expertise. Early in my career, I needed widgets made, but the Applied Research Department didn't have a dedicated model shop. My manager introduced me to the head machinist in the physics model shop. He checked me out on a few machines, found me competent, and allowed me to use the equipment. He gave me a refresher course if necessary, before turning me loose each time. I could create what I had in my head much faster in Plexiglas than by trying to draw properly on graph paper.

Almost everything I wanted to create had at least one challenging piece, such as a 10 mil (0.010 inches) hole through a half inch of Plexiglas. For each new project, I described my widget to the head machinist. He encouraged me to do everything else, and then he drilled the hole for me. He never failed.

The head machinist never affected my promotions. He couldn't refer me to the next and more challenging job. He could, however, make it easier for me to do my job. Between us, we could create whatever widgets I needed. His friendship contributed to my success.

Nominate someone

Nominating someone for an award says you respect them and you have noticed their work. Of course, if you don't bother to join a professional organization, you may not have the opportunity to nominate anyone, so this is one more reason to join.

My nominator for the National Academy of Engineering (NAE) knew me through informal evening hikes arranged by volunteers in our company, and through local Sigma Xi lectures twenty-five years previously. We had worked in related areas, but never on the same project.

My assistant brought me a large package on a Thursday afternoon in February 2004. In today's environment, you check the return address rather than thoughtlessly opening an unexpected package. When I saw it was from the NAE, all I could think was, "Rejections don't come in big packages." Sure enough, the package contained a congratulatory letter and an invitation to the invocation for me and a guest. The membership book was also inside.

The next morning my first e-mail was a congratulatory note about my NAE election from one of the IEEE Fellow references I had contacted for a colleague I was nominating. I thanked him by e-mail and asked if he would be at the invocation. He sent back, "I'm chair of the peer committee that processed your nomination. I have to attend."

During this time, I organized the IEEE Fellow nomination for a colleague. Her references included outside people I had never met nor even heard of. Without those references, the nomination would not be considered. After my election, I discovered three of her eight references evaluated my NAE nomination. Although the first attempt was unsuccessful, we knew the second try was many times more likely to succeed. We tried again and the second time was successful.

If you build a solid network, the benefits will amaze you. You will be able to nominate others for honors they richly deserve, and your nominations will carry weight because people know you. You will receive honors you never imagined. You will have friends to call upon if you find yourself looking for a new job, and you will find you have connections with thousands of people you've never met.

Your Job is Changing

If you don't understand that your job will always be changing, you are asking for unpleasant surprises. During my early years in Research, the emphasis seemed to change every year. One year the push was for external papers. The following year the emphasis was on invention and submitting invention disclosures. Next, it might be technology transfer. Finally, I realized the emphasis would never stabilize. It's all important. The most recently stressed areas are in the best shape, so they fall to the bottom of the queue and something else requires more attention.

Commitment to life-long learning

Every professional needs to make a life-long commitment to learning. One of my aunts said, "I'm still trying to figure out what I'm going to be when I grow up." She was at least 75 when I heard her make this statement. Statistics indicate most professionals will change fields several times in their career. If you are not keeping up to date, you are likely to become redundant. My first two years with the company I worked with different technologies every few months. I tried experiments to leave marks on paper using chemistry, surface tension (physics), ultrasonics, thermal, and various other technologies. By the time I switched into data compression (by accident), I was ready to stabilize. I'm one of the rare people who did not change fields every five years. However, that doesn't stop me from interacting with people in a number of other fields.

One of my co-workers is an amazing example of continual—and mostly self-taught—learning on the job. He earned his PhD in low temperature physics, and accepted a job in that field. The program was terminated before he started work. Instead of low temperature physics, he worked on displays. He taught himself circuits and programming. He did state-of-the-art RF sputtering using his low temperature skills. Then he became involved in printing. We started to work together on the internal teleconferencing system in 1980. He was elemental in making arithmetic coding practical. Together, we were co-editors in JPEG and we wrote the JPEG book together. When he retired in 1993, he learned LaTeX (a composition tool) and became an expert in the internet. We wrote the MPEG book using his new tools. At that time, he told me the course of our work in image processing and data compression was the longest he had stayed in one field during his long career. Since then he has connected a small lathe to his computer and he creates toy furniture. Without a commitment to learning, he would not have enjoyed the success he did.

Master your material; learn for the sake of learning

Sometime late in elementary school, one of my teachers compared learning to surfing. If you master the previous material, a little bit of new learning (paddling) will allow you to catch the wave and then the wave carries you along. Surfing/Learning is fun and you get excellent results. However, if you are missing background, it's like missing the wave. The effort to catch up to the wave is unlikely to succeed and you work hard without any fruits or fun to show for your labors. Whenever you are tempted to skip learning new material, remind yourself you don't want to miss the wave. It's easier and more fun to learn things the first time than to have to catch up later.

My freshman year in college everyone had to take a course in western civilization. My teaching assistant was an older man. He had been a Professor of Geology in Hungary and fled the country during the revolution. More than a decade later, he was working on a PhD in history in order to understand what happened to his country. He told us, "They can take the piece of sheepskin away; they can't take what you learned away." His words had a profound influence on me, reinforcing my determination to work for mastery rather than for a grade.

If you stay the same, you are slipping behind

During my second or third year at Research, I attended a seminar in which an outside expert contended that it is human nature to expect people to grow in their jobs. Then he showed a graph in which years in a given job were plotted versus perceived quality of work. The slope was negative. He explained this comes from the gap between the expectation that a person will keep growing and the reality that they have not improved on the job.

There is a natural progression through stages every time a person switches into a new technical discipline. He labeled the four stages as apprentice, independent worker, manager, and executive. He identified the relationship between a graduate student and his thesis advisor as a research apprenticeship. The process of becoming a deep technical expert in one's chosen field during a worker's early years in industry reflects that of an independent worker. A manager is someone who influences the work scope of multiple people. An executive is expected to have good judgment outside of his original field.

Then he urged a technical promotion ladder not requiring people-management for top technical talent, so they don't need to transfer to the management chain in order to influence others' work and eventually become executives. He outlined expressions of this progression in responsibility. For example, a person can grow to influence the team, the department, the division, and the company. Additionally, someone can have influence at the local level, at the state level, at the national level and finally at the international level. Similarly, the individual can be respected and have an impact within their own company, then within their industry locally, nationally within a broader definition of their industry, and finally across multiple industries.

Participation in external professional societies is one way to gain increased leadership responsibility without people-management. An apprentice attends a conference to learn about a new field, the independent worker gives a paper sharing his original work, the manager organizes a session in his expertise for the external organization, and the executive organizes the whole conference spanning multiple fields.

Another progression would have the apprentice begin by attending local chapter meetings of professional organizations. The independent worker volunteers to work on a committee. The manager chairs the committee, and the executive is president of the local chapter and keeps track of multiple committees. Another growth path moves from local chapter officer, to society officer, to parent organization officer, and finally to officer in a collection of professional organizations worldwide.

The key point is that everyone needs to accept additional responsibilities and continue to grow and widen their job definition or they may become dead wood.

Productivity

Tom DeMarco's book, *PeopleWare*, deals with creating physical environments to improve the productivity of software developers. However, the book suggests factors of five in code generation productivity are possible when software coders write for the joy of sharing the results with their peer group rather than under deadlines. I was not impressed with the rigor behind the experimental data, but the book had some valid points.

Learning to grow in your career requires significant self-examination. You need to understand the environment that makes you happiest and most productive. You need to understand the working style that makes you happiest and most productive. And at the same time, you need to understand these things about your colleagues. When you're happy, you are productive. When you are unhappy, or uncomfortable, productivity becomes a struggle.

Some people find music increases their productivity. The background of melodic sound allows your mind to find the 'zone' of productivity, and you sail through your work almost without effort. And of course, those who like music while they work have specific taste in music. Some want the energy and rhythm of rock and roll, others need the heavy beat of rap, while still others seek the complex chords of classical. Only you know what speaks to your heart and allows you to enjoy your work.

Some people find music—or sound of any kind—to be distracting. For these people, the soaring notes of opera create an environment that makes work impossible. Some of them find themselves caught up in the music, while others find the music just so much distracting noise.

If music helps you think, by all means enjoy your music. But keep in mind that what helps you may distract others around you. Keep your productivity enhancers contained so they don't become productivity inhibitors for others.

In the same vein, as mentioned before, some people need constant interaction with others in order to increase their productivity. Others need quiet and the opportunity to work uninterrupted. Be cognizant of the needs of your colleagues so that you do not shine at their expense.

Some people thrive on the opportunity not only to solve the problem, but also to identify the problem. Others take a clearly identified problem and sail through to a viable solution in moments. Which kind are you? If you examine yourself honestly, you will probably find you are a little of both, and over time, your preference for one situation or the other changes. You grow in your career.

Multiplexing tends to increase my productivity. If I get stuck, or want time to think about one project, having another waiting for my attention helps. Sometimes I deliberately schedule writing a paper concurrently with writing an invention disclosure. I switch easily. This is not true for everyone. It is important to notice the working styles of your teammates so you can play to their strengths.

One of my colleagues hates interruptions. For years, I couldn't understand why he became annoyed when I bounced in several times a day to ask questions, share a new idea, or involve him in further brainstorming. Finally, I realized he meant it when he said, "I lose at least an hour of work because I have to start completely over at the task I was working on." To solve the problem, I used my Daytimer to write down each of my questions. My colleague agreed to stop by my office after he picked up his afternoon coffee. He would give me his attention as he relaxed and drank his coffee. You must allow others to find their groove and accommodate different working styles.

Learn to identify and remove productivity inhibitors

My second year in New York, I car-pooled to work. I enjoyed not having to drive in the wintry ice and snow. However, the others in our group were non-exempt workers. This meant they had to be at work on time and had to leave on time. Remembering to leave on time became a productivity inhibitor for me. I didn't dare work on the interesting stuff after 4 PM for fear I would keep my car-pool waiting. I became so engrossed in work I was oblivious to the time. My car-pool limited my productivity.

Study your working situation. Are you limiting your productivity or that of others around you? Do you chatter incessantly when someone else is trying to work? Make appointments with them to talk so you have the opportunity to ask questions and share ideas, and they have quiet time to work. Does your colleague's blaring rock and roll distract you? Ask him to use a headset. Do you get so caught up in work that time escapes you? Get an alarm clock to remind you when it's time to meet your ride. Look for creative solutions to work related problems. Give yourself an environment conducive to productivity.

Sometimes moving slow is a good sign

It took me years to realize productivity is not necessarily tied to speed. I've been known to take two hours to eat breakfast—normally a twenty minute task. Sometimes I move slowly and don't have any idea why, but within a few hours—a few days at most—I have a major breakthrough on something. While I'm poking along appearing to do nothing, and wondering why I can't seem to move faster, my mind is working furiously on something important. I just don't know what that something important is. Nowadays when I realize I'm being more lethargic than usual, I acknowledge the inefficiency and expect something wonderful in the near future. Of course, 'moving slow' doesn't mean reading the paper or magazines instead of showering and dressing for work. 'Moving slow' means being physically in slow motion, lethargic, catching myself wondering what in the world I was in the middle of doing.

When you find yourself unable to concentrate, or unwilling to move at your normal speed, acknowledge it and forget it. Your mind is at work. Your mind multitasks, even when you don't realize what it's doing. You are working steadily away at your project, and you suddenly remember Junior's soccer game next Saturday, or a balding spot on the right front tire. It's just multitasking. But sometimes your unconscious mind is so busy with a problem that it takes up more of your mental and physical resources than usual. Expect great things.

Set expectations

I was in Marketing for almost three years. The most important thing I learned from it was to set expectations. I make sure people know half my 'brilliant ideas' don't work. I just try to figure out which half quickly. This allows me to take bigger risks and not have to keep new projects secret until I can prove they work.

My first manager encouraged working 50 percent on your main project, and 25 percent on your back burner project. Your back burner project is your next project—the one you need to have ready to go if you stall on the main project. He said he didn't need to know how you spent the final 25 percent of your time. Of course, not all managers feel this way. If you don't work in research, your time may all be committed to specific tasks. If your job doesn't lend itself to running several projects simultaneously, set aside thinking time somewhere else in your day. Allowing your mind to wander increases productivity.

First steps into data compression

Sometimes, the only way to increase your productivity is to change your job. I've already told you how I made a decision to kill my projects when I believed they had no hope of success. It is a waste of time and energy—and company resources—to continue working on something that will never succeed. It is equally wasteful to spend your time and energy on projects for which you have no joy or passion. Only you can decide if your situation requires this kind of change, and you may lose your job over it, so move cautiously.

I was fortunate. I shared a data compression idea with my manager. After agreeing that I'd return to ultrasonic printing, I asked for a week to test my ideas. I wanted to use it as an excuse to talk to other researchers and get out of the habit of isolation. He suggested several names of people who had been in our recent printing course. On Monday morning, a safety issue arose within the labs, which made normal lab work impossible and freed me up to follow my passion. After the first evidence came back positive, my manager took me to meet with the second line manager.

My decision to take the initiative made a tremendous difference in my career. With the increased interaction, I was happier, and it's much easier to be productive when you're happy. I took the initiative to increase my network, which gave me more visibility within the company. And I learned things. I learned other people were interested in what I was doing and what I had to say, and I learned other people knew things I needed to know. With more interaction, work became a joy once more.

The world has changed since I entered the field of data compression. If you work in research, you may not have the same sort of freedom I enjoyed. I chose many of my projects. But once I found my passion, I would have followed it against all opposition. You have the freedom to do the same.

One way to increase your freedom is to change your working schedule. Most people work days, which means the equipment you need in order to pursue your passion may be in use during the day. Try working at night. Obviously, you can't do this without permission, but you can't get permission without asking. Many of my mentees work extra hours in order to have the freedom to pursue their passions. Many of them work weekends. If you truly have a passion for something, you can find a way to pursue it.

Many people unconsciously fear success even more than they fear failure. Don't let the fear of success stop you from succeeding. Back when I was working on the fax standard, I woke up one night in a cold sweat. If I succeeded, I would have to attend the standards meeting in Geneva, Switzerland. I hadn't even been to a *conference* in the field of data compression. The fear nearly paralyzed me. Eventually, I remembered the lecture on the stages of becoming an expert and thought, "Someday I will influence the world, so this is just getting started early." You want to influence the world. Recognize the fear, and let it go. Don't let it paralyze you into non-action.

Simplify

"If it doesn't start simple, forget it because it's only going to get more complicated."
One of my colleagues in data compression taught me this mantra. Every level of complexity adds to the possibility of errors. Every level of complexity adds to the explanation you must supply when you try to sell your idea to your manager or your colleagues, or the customer. If you think about it, most technological advances are an attempt to simplify. Simplicity sells, and sales are what pay our salaries and enable us to follow our passions.

Other people will follow in your footsteps; using the systems you develop, or building the widgets you develop, or implementing the code you write. If you create complexity, you lessen the chances they will be able to do so successfully. You want to influence the world. Make it possible for others to follow.

Document what you create. This is back to writing, which you already know to be an essential business skill. Our internal teleconferencing system code had almost no comments. This was one of my first major code projects and I couldn't imagine forgetting what the code did. We received criticism on our weak documentation when we transferred the code to another division for implementation. It was a legitimate complaint, so we went back and commented almost every line of code—a task requiring almost three months. If you don't comment your code as you go along, you can expect to do it later, after you've forgotten what you thought you'd never forget.

If you don't happen to be a programmer, document whatever you do. If the doctor fails to note down the diagnosis and the treatment, the nurse has no clear instructions. If the physical fitness trainer fails to list your daily regimen, you don't know what to do. If the salesman fails to write down the order, the customer doesn't receive his shipment. Whatever your job, you need to keep good records. Without records, you have no defense when life deals you lemons.

Proper documentation saves other people time and energy, which increases their productivity. They don't have to re-invent. I asked a senior engineer, "Why are you mucking around in these bits and bytes, when there are clearly defined parameters in the interface to your code which allows you to set a parameter and the code will run much faster." He hadn't been aware documentation existed. I located a decade-old version and a few hours later, he had his code running much faster and using much less memory.

Sometimes productivity requires slogging through long hours of seemingly pointless work. Toward the end of the Geneva fax standards meeting, the ad hoc decided the different algorithms should be tested for error resilience. My lab had a high quality printer so I volunteered to print the error images. I had already learned those who work have more power.

I estimated I would receive no more than twenty-four error images from the standards delegates. By the time all the new proposals came in, we were committed to over a hundred. I asked for help and accepted the assistance of a post-doc only after I knew his permanent job offer was in the works. I told him he would be working with data compression experts from all over the world and the grunt work could be useful for his career. The young man did the work reluctantly.

It did not occur to me to do anything but work the long hours necessary to support our proposal. I later learned the three of us did more work to support the standard than an eight-person team with a several million-dollar budget working in another country. All techniques were basically unable to recover from errors, and our proposal gained extra credibility because we had been willing to put in the work. After this experience, I realized I should have declared the numbers beyond our capacity and unilaterally decided to print the same two images for each proposal in order to bring it back into the agreed upon range. Next time. And again, communication is critical. Never assume.

You should write a paper now

My temporary manager was pleased with the results of the Geneva meeting and ordered me to write a paper about our proposal in the next two weeks. The paper was for a conference and was already overdue. I just looked at him and burst into tears. I was scheduled to leave for Christmas vacation the next day. I was tired and knew I needed to regroup. To my surprise, he promptly apologized and said he forgot he was both my first and second-line manager. He wasn't thinking like my first line manager. He asked if I could create the paper in the week after my vacation, then called the conference chair and arranged for the paper to arrive late. That paper was actually fun to write after I'd had my vacation.

Finding your passion

With my introduction to data compression, I found my passion, and having found what mattered most to me, and what I could be best at, I began to manage my career. I met with my manager and proposed that I be released from a project that had no joy for me, and assigned instead to a field of research rich with opportunity. This is true freedom.

It's All Politics

Being ignorant of local politics and company culture is a good recipe for long-term dissatisfaction. Corporate advancement is not an accident; it comes from knowing what is needed and preparing in advance for the next step.

'Politics' is not a dirty word

After participating in international standards I realized politics is the art of convincing others that it is in their best interests to do exactly what you want done. This definition served me well on the JPEG committee. Democracy is not the most efficient system, but it encourages participation by everyone and gives people opportunities to stretch and grow. This knowledge significantly increased my patience and willingness to give people (including myself) time to grow.

Before I learned to understand politics, my reaction was a desire to run far away. What helped me stop running was realizing I was not obliged to play the game by someone else's rules. I could choose not to play the game. I couldn't choose not to know what game was being played. Actually, you *can* choose not to know what game is being played if you don't care whether you are stepping on toes. It made sense to me to understand when I was offending people instead of doing it unintentionally.

Whatever your job, wherever you work, you will be subject to office politics. You can avoid becoming a political target by doing nothing. If you never produce anything of note, never draw attention to yourself in any way, never strive for a promotion, or express an opinion, you can probably go through life under the political radar. Since you want to change the world, that isn't an option for you.

Office politics includes 'dirty tricks'

The first time I visited Boulder, I discovered I had been set up. Another data compression expert from the lab on the other coast was scheduled for the same room. Our host had set us up to compete with each without informing us in advance. My talk delayed his data compression presentation on hardware chips. The other guy was more than a little annoyed. In front of everyone, he asked our mutual host, "How come you're paying for Joan's visit and not for mine?" The host replied, "I'm not paying for Joan's visit." I barely managed not to cry. The only reason I'd been allowed to come was on the assurance the Research Division was not paying.

Fortunately, my old manager invited me to dinner at his home. When he got home, he told me not to worry about it. I didn't. Boulder paid. This is a good time to remind you of the importance of communication. Never assume.

If you are accomplishing great things, you are threatening someone else. You may be threatening another project, or only another person, but greatness always threatens mediocrity. If you are unaware of politics, you may be blind-sided, as I was in Boulder. On the other hand, if you pay attention to what happens around you, you have some warning of what may come. In either case, take dirty tricks for what they are—a sign you are on the right track.

Corporate politics serve a purpose

At IBM, in order to propose a CCITT standard, such as the fax standard, you must convince a division to use the technology if the standard is accepted. This makes a lot of sense if you think about it. No company wants to devote resources to a project they can't use. If the divisions won't buy into a way of doing something, the only thing the company gets for their expenditure is the 'glory' of proposing the standard. In the case of the fax standard, we agreed to name the standard after the Japanese proposal, so IBM didn't even get the glory.

Politics can interfere with projects

In 1980, a small team of us at Research linked up with another division to put together an internal teleconferencing system. This was a freeze-frame system designed for cooperative collaboration between engineers rather than executive negotiations. We wanted a system we could afford to use around the world. Another division decided we were infringing on their turf. They had designed a system using a much lower resolution camera. Since they had corporate headquarters on their side, we were expected to attend three-day monthly meetings at their site at Research expense. We couldn't understand why we couldn't conduct these meetings using the teleconferencing system already partially deployed. This continued for over a year.

Finally, headquarters called a week-long meeting at their site to decide if I could write code (estimated as a two week job) to allow interconnection between the two systems. I refused to attend. I acknowledged they had the right to decide to deploy the code, but I intended to create the proof of concept and not waste time in their meeting. The meeting was not held. The work took a month, including the testing time, and the code deployed without further debate. I wish we had realized we had the power to refuse to attend months earlier.

One of the long-term arguments had been whether the quality of a 320 x 240 camera was the same as the quality of a 512 x 480 camera. To my team, this was like arguing that gravity is different in some places. The other team claimed to have shown it to be true experimentally (the camera resolution, not gravity). When we deployed, a bug was found in the code because the 512 x 480 camera they used for their experiments had no data in the second field. Poor equipment led them to bad science.

Sometimes what appears to be a political battle is not political

Sibling rivalry between the east and west coast research laboratories was not unknown on projects. In my field of data compression, about the time the facsimile data compression standard was being frozen, the other laboratory was making major breakthroughs allowing the use of adaptive (dynamic) probabilities rather than stationary (static) statistics. I tried to act as the communicator and visited the West Coast Laboratory at least once a year while in California on vacation.

I knew if we didn't resolve our differences, the company would implement neither option. We were convinced their technique would slow the software by a factor of two. They in turn, were convinced our incompatible approach penalized the hardware throughput a factor of two. This went on for years, so you can imagine my chagrin when I finally understood it wasn't a political game on their part (and surely not on ours), but a genuine technical problem.

That night I lay on the futon bed on my sister's floor praying. We needed a solution that was good for both hardware and software. I knew a solution existed. Sometime after midnight, I remembered a brain teaser. How do you remove a dollar bill from underneath a full glass of water without spilling the water and without moving the glass? To this day, the memory is in pictures—not words. The solution is to tear the bill in half as you pull equally on both sides. That memory triggered another picture; you can approach a point on a number line from two directions. I was so excited I could hardly sleep. I ran through the two processes allowing the hardware and the software to take their optimal (and different) approaches and yet arrive at compatible answers. It took another six months to understand why we got to *identical* data streams rather than *compatible* data streams, but from then on, the two projects worked together for a common solution that would allow the hardware and software to take different approaches to the same point.

Company cultures

Company cultures are often set during the company's formative years. The book, *The Winning Performance*, found a positive correlation between start-ups that begin in warehouses with leaking roofs and ultimate success. The book concluded frugality enters into the company culture. The opposite is true for companies who put a lot of money into prestigious premises and furniture.

The following are theories I have developed over many years. They help me to analyze the local culture. It is important to understand cultures can change radically as you move around within a company. They can even change between groups in the same department. These ideas are not scientifically proven theories.

During the Middle Ages, the only defense barons had against their neighbors was the king. If the king withdrew his support, rivals could claim their lands and take or kill their families. It was a brutal world. Making the king look bad was treasonous and could be lethal. This hierarchical world model encouraged politics that looked upward for help and protection. History has many examples of such models. The Israelites demanded a king so they could be like their neighbors. Even though they had been warned he would take their sons and their daughters, they clamored for a king. So they got Saul.

The first time I noticed hierarchical models of company structure was when I started my job. With some people, you could just drop in. Others wanted formal appointments. Job titles didn't always give you a clue. I designated the 'kingmaker' model for those cases where a person seemed to think his job was to keep his manager happy and looking good. The kingmaker looks up the management chain. Individuals who thrive in this environment are often ambitious for themselves, and they take every opportunity to interact upwards. There is nothing wrong with interacting upwards, until no one is minding the store downwards.

Strongly hierarchical models require you to follow the 'chain of command'. If you work within a hierarchical structure, you must follow protocol. Going over your manager's head may subject you to disciplinary action. Or it may subject you to a level of 'dirty tricks' that you cannot overcome. Taking your problem to your boss's boss makes your boss look bad, because he or she was not able to control your actions. And if the boss's boss agrees with your position, you have also made your boss 'wrong'. Of course if your company culture is based on what used to be called the 'old boys' network' you may find a new sponsor this way, but you are more likely to find yourself in political hot water.

A second model is the Servant/Shepherd. The Shepherd looks after his sheep. He tends them, and makes certain they have good food, and peaceful waters. He defends them against predators and others who would steal them away. I characterize this as looking down. The Shepherd makes sure the workers have what they need to do their jobs. The Shepherd is more other-motivated than self-motivated. The classic example of this model in the modern world is the owner of the start-up who can be found sweeping the floors. I believe successful new businesses must begin with this model or the business is unlikely to be run efficiently.

For years, I thought the Shepherd/Servant model was the only correct one, particularly after I learned that a Roman Centurion (commander of about a 100 troops) faced execution if he lost 60 percent of his fighting men. Every centurion was powerfully motivated to see that his men had good training, food, shelter, and sleep. His success—and his life—hinged on them doing well.

In recent years, I realized both models are necessary, and can coexist. The king sees the bigger picture and pays attention to long-term strategy. The kingmaker deals up the chain to obtain necessary resources. Meanwhile, the shepherd pays attention to details and the needs of the employees. Military organizations are hierarchical in nature, with each lower level answering upwards and controlling downwards. At the lowest levels, though, the non-commissioned officer takes on the role of Shepherd, caring for his troops and making sure they have the training and equipment necessary to do their jobs.

All company cultures rely on networks of friends and acquaintances. By now, you understand the importance of networks. John knows Don, and knows that Don is an expert at analysis, so when the company/division/department/team has need of outstanding analytical skills, John recommends Don. Mary knows Sally to be an excellent negotiator, so when her department faces a tough negotiating situation, Mary calls upon Sally's expertise. Networks make the running of companies easier and more successful. In a very few cases, who you know is more important than competence. If this seems to be the case in your situation, call upon your mentors. Make sure you have your facts correct. You may be misreading a situation.

Learn to recognize the 'movers, shakers, and influencers.' If you understand the local power structure and culture, you can leverage your knowledge and understanding to accomplish your goals. Otherwise, you will miss the decision makers and waste time on the executors. The person who talks loudest is probably not the one who makes things happen. Talkers like to think the world revolves around them, but they rarely cause much to happen. It is important, on every new project and in every situation, to figure out who makes the decisions and who has the most influence. Often the key people don't appear to be very high on the organization chart, but people listen to them and they wield a great deal of influence. The relationships can be complicated, but learning to understand them can also be fun if you treat it as a technical challenge and keep your eyes open. If you want to make things happen, be observant and don't take people at their own evaluation. You should not only check to see if what they say is what they do, but also if the names they drop ever listen to them. This is another good time to call upon your mentors. Share your observations with them and ask for confirmation of your conclusions.

Having learned to recognize the powerful people, I strongly recommend you don't start a political fight you can't win. If you are going to fight, figure out in advance how to win quickly so nobody gets hurt. Recognizing who has the power to influence can help you win quickly. A word from an influencer may stop the battle before it begins. Once battle lines are drawn, it is difficult to find a path to lasting peace.

Before you escalate an issue, put on your 'think like an owner' hat. As an owner, decide, "Is this escalation worthy of the company's time and resources?" If not, drop it while you can gracefully exit. There are few things worse than creating a big stink and then discovering the issue isn't really important.

The politics of getting along

Turn people you think of as 'they' into people you think of as 'we'. Look for things to admire in people with whom you do not get along. After a while, you won't see the fault that once seemed important. I did this with an individual I worked with in Burlington while on leave of absence. Years later, I learned he had figured out how to continue my quarter-time pay by arranging to have Burlington pay Research to pay me.

Thank people for their constructive criticism. As previously mentioned, a competitive group criticized our teleconferencing system excessively. We had specified long persistence phosphors for the displays, but they were no longer available, and short persistence phosphors were substituted. After installation, we received a strongly worded memo complaining about graphics flicker, so we visited a room nearby. The screen was so bad I could hardly stand to look at it. Two weeks later, we had written fast code, invented, and installed a solution. We replied to the memo thanking them for exposing a major problem and telling them the solution had been installed. The author of the previous memo saw the solution and wrote another memo supporting our system and withdrawing previous objections. Years later, we met and worked well together, something we would not have been able to do if either of us had held onto inharmonious feelings.

What do you do when your actions are causing uproar? Most great new things come about despite opposition from groups satisfied with the status quo. Mom used to say, "When there's a big upset, you must be doing something right." At first, I didn't understand her reasoning. Later I realized big uproars don't happen over mediocre things. They happen because something is important. So a big upset may be a positive sign and not a negative sign. Consult with neutral friends to find out what it is that's causing the fuss. You may be on the right track, and this is when it's important to zig and zag rather than quit. Beware the biased friend in cases like this. Their advice may steer you wrong.

Of course, I've known people who measure your sincerity by your persistence, so the worst thing you can do is believe their first, "No." They may intend to change their answer as soon as they are convinced you're serious. The best way to figure this out is to observe their behavior with other people when you are not emotionally involved. It's easy to see if the "No" is just part of a game when you're only an outside observer.

Most of us have had 'friends' try to discourage us from a particular research project, and then when it nears fruition, offer to help. You can tell when someone is trying to position themselves to claim glory. I've found it effective to say, "Yes, I welcome your help. There is so much work to get this finished. Which piece do you want to own? Having your help to get the work done will be great!" As you rave about all the *work*, you can watch them back away. Politically, this is much more polite than frankly telling them "No." "No" gets their defenses up and makes an enemy unnecessarily.

Make it easy for people to say yes without having to say it. When my third line manager stepped in to get the proposal 'cleared' for the Geneva standard meeting, he used a technique I had never seen before. With each person he called, he asked for the 'yes', but he went on to explain if they said 'no', they had to give him reasons to pass along to his boss. Then he pointed out they didn't really care, so they should just agree. He also taught me to put the question so no action gave the desired result. For example, "If I don't hear from you by this date (mm/dd/yy), I'll do ...." Usually you don't hear, so it works.

When you have difficulties, you worry about it, and worries get in your way. My mother taught me two ways to turn worries over to God. In one, she pretended she was on a cruise ship. She went to the back of the ship where she saw the wake. Then she took out her worries and carefully threw them overboard. She did this as she prayed, "Please God, if you want me to do something about this, send it back, and show me what to do." Another image she shared was to take all her worries and carefully tie them up in a sheet the way people used to do with dirty laundry. Then she mentally tossed the whole bundle up to God and said, "Okay God, if I'm supposed to do something, let me know. If necessary, hit me over the head with a two by four so I can't miss it. And of course, you will need to show me what to do."

My life became much less complicated when I realized that after praying I feel at peace. It isn't my job to be God. I don't have to correct the Universe. My job is to correct my own thinking and then be about my business. I can let God tell the other person whatever He wants them to know.

Study politics so you can understand the games

I received *Hardball for Women*, by Pat Heim, as an attendee of a conference in Boulder for about one hundred company women. Ms. Heim conducted one of the sessions. Her book summarizes *Games Your Mother Never Taught You* without recommending you play the games. Pat encourages professionals to set limits on their adaptation to the dominant culture, a recommendation I appreciated. She also makes clear some of the unwritten rules, and has useful suggestions on how to deal with corporate environments. I recommend it to everyone, female and male.

Until I heard Pat Heim talk about her 'dead even power rule', I never understood how much cultural expectations for females colored my view of reality. As she explains it, women tend to cooperate and want equality. Thousands of years ago, women in the later months of pregnancy couldn't run as fast as their unburdened sisters. If they didn't band together and help each other, their survival rate dropped. So women learned to cooperate and accept lateral equality. On the other hand, men jockey for position and try to move up in the pecking order. They want to know where they fit in the scheme of things. Men needed the protection of more important men, and in turn, they protected those who didn't challenge their superior position. This led to the hierarchical model with an 'up' and a 'down' rather than lateral equality.

Finding your political style

My first manager used to tell me to stop saying thank you so much. He insisted it was counterproductive to thank the secretary for doing the job she was paid to do. I asked several different secretaries for the name of a female manager whom they respected. They all named the same person, so I made an appointment and had a discussion. I was amazed at how many of my actions were not conducive to getting the service I needed. She recommended I always write a Post-It in which I included the due date and my priority. Then I should let the secretaries come to me with questions rather than burdening them with extra details.

Years later, I had opportunity to talk to the secretary away from work and ask her about some of the points I had learned. She remembered the positive change in behavior and wondered what happened.

When you can't solve the problem, document it

My phone was supposed to be answered, and I tried to tell my manager I was not receiving that service. Finally, the telephone was just one more thing telling me it was time to move to another job. After the new job had been arranged, my manager came to my office one evening and asked for my help to run an experiment with the phones. I called my phone from his office. He stood at the empty secretarial station and watched the phone lights. Nothing happened. Then he listened while I told him I had been getting messages from overseas calls for the past six months, but not from domestic calls. Dad had told me he liked the new arrangement because I was the only person who ever answered my phone. I never knew when my number disappeared from the secretary's phone.

My mistake was making oral complaints to my manager, but not following up with a written memo. I had no paper trail. I should have sent him an e-mail (and maybe even copied the secretary) informing him I would keep records of my phone messages and the phone calls I answered. If I had documented the problem properly, the secretary would have been forced to address my issues, and the fact that my line didn't show up on her desk would have been discovered. If I had documented the problem, my manager would have been moved to investigate long before frustration drove me to request a transfer. If you don't properly document your problems, you deny people the opportunity to address them.

Politics and negotiation

The second standards meeting I attended was in Japan and by this time I understood more about negotiating—but no more about politics. During the meeting, if I sat down alone for lunch at the conference center, a delegate from a Japanese company would ask to join me. They had a common mantra, "You can't win, but don't cave in. We need the compromise." Thinking this was a technical discussion, I asked for some technical reasons to accept the British compromise. I got some shaking of heads and occasionally the honest answer, "It is political, and not technical." Several years later, I looked back and realized it had all been orchestrated.

No one ever said an unkind word, but I picked up a strong sense of, "You are not needed here," and, "You are slowing up the process, why don't you disappear." I held to my understanding that Principle/God was in charge even when circumstances screamed otherwise.

After more than a week of examining the proposals from the basis of the requirements and finally focusing in on three, all progress seemed to stop. At first, nothing could be touched in the Japanese proposal, and then one day everything was up for negotiation. Eventually, the Japanese submitted a document saying they would accept a compromise as long as the final solution was named after their proposal.

Once the Japanese got most of the credit, the second requirement of the compromise was that all companies make their patents available without fees. Since this is what everyone had been working toward, people were happy to agree to this requirement. The Japanese finally agreed—in writing—not to assert their patent against people implementing the standard.

Once I learned to understand politics, negotiating became easier. The second convener of JPEG accused my company's salesmen of things that were firing offenses under our internal ethics rules. I told him my company had announced—in the paper—they would sell his company their high speed memory chips until the market prices for high speed memory returned to normal levels. This allowed his company to announce and ship their latest machine. By the next meeting, his antagonism had permanently disappeared. I had learned the benefits of using politics.

Titles

Titles serve many purposes. They identify power positions, both inside and outside the company. They are frequently used to reward employees—often in lieu of a raise. Beware the company that offers you an impressive sounding title without the resources, pay, and authority to go with it.

I heard of a start-up founder who carried around multiple business cards. Some cards carried his true position as founder and CEO of the company. Other cards claimed he was the Vice President of whatever. He used the less impressive title when he didn't want to be pressed for a decision. He could claim he had to check with the CEO before committing to a deal. Be aware this kind of subterfuge may be used on you. If you do your homework, the game doesn't work. All the cards had his real name, so anyone who did their research would have known his true position.

The internet makes doing your homework much easier. Being knowledgeable about a company is a way to demonstrate the company is important to you. Would you want to deal with a salesman who doesn't know what your business does? Showing a genuine interest gets you off to a good start.

Don't let an interest in politics derail your career. You have to understand the culture you work in, but the job is not to play politics. The job is to research, develop, hire, manage, build, or whatever. I met a new employee who was fascinated by politics and very astute. We always talked politics instead of having long technical discussions and I wonder if I did him a disservice. He never settled down as an independent researcher. He left after a few years and has done well in academia.

Writing about the politics has been a walk down memory lane for me. In graduate school, I was aware such things went on around me, but I ignored them. I assumed I could do the same thing in business. It didn't work on standards committees and it doesn't work in business if you want to make things happen. Don't make my mistakes. Pay attention and learn to leverage the system to get things done. This is literally the 'area I want to improve' on my yearly evaluation form.

It's your career, manage it

Sometimes the hardest thing to do is to stop being comfortable and branch out into the unknown. If our job is to be the best we can be and help others around us to be the best that they can be, then at some point 'comfortable' is headed for stagnation. It may be time to move on. You must work your way out of jobs. Train the people around you to do your job. If you want to have opportunities and be able to change positions, you need to train your replacement(s). Being indispensable is not job security; it's a trap.

I still remember the advice I received in my time management class. "The fastest way to read a book is to decide in the first five minutes that the book is not worth reading." This advice applies to most things in life. Some projects may not be worth doing. Why write a white paper if someone else has already done a better job? If you don't start out by looking, you will never know. So before you invest any effort, ask yourself, "Can I find this already done somewhere?"

Summary

- Understand your company culture
- Make it easy for your manager to do what you want
- Your job will change; grow with it
- Learn how and when you are most productive and capitalize on your strengths
- Learn to enjoy politics, both in and out of the office

5

Be a Mentor

$\mathcal{M}$entoring is sharing your expertise with someone less skilled. You can have both a mentor and a mentee relationship with the same person as long as you are each more skilled than the other in some area.

This advice probably won't work for people who believe knowledge is power and only want to share their knowledge in exchange for immediate benefits. You aren't one of those people. You understand the benefit of sharing knowledge.

Since I have appreciated others noticing me and offering to help in some way (for example, nominating me for some honor or award), I don't hesitate to offer to mentor others. However, I often open a relationship with something vague such as, "How would you like to join me for lunch next Tuesday?" If we have an interesting lunch, I can encourage them further with, "This has certainly been helpful to me. If you are interested, I'd be happy to officially mentor you."

I've already told you my mentoring rule, "I'm the mentor. I get to make all the suggestions I want. You are the mentee. It is your life. As long as you convince me you understand the suggestions, you are free to ignore them. After all, it is your life."

When I want to make mentoring suggestions, I find it helps to tell people, "Please put on your mentee hat." This makes it clear our conversation has left the technical realm and is moving into the personal. If you have a good mentoring relationship, it is usually safe to make strong recommendations for improvement of interpersonal skills without offending the other person. Outside the mentor relationship, personal criticism, no matter how well-intentioned, can be dangerous.

Leadership and mentoring

As you remember from previous stories, the job is always changing. One way to get ready for the next change (and to manage your career) is to start mentoring now. You will be surprised how often you learn more than you feel you taught during a mentoring conversation. You observe more carefully when you know you will be asked for feedback. Some of the things you notice will be what they are doing right, and you may discover ways to improve yourself. You observe what happens around you more closely when you know someone else will ask you questions about the company culture. Those questions may open your eyes to things you failed to notice.

One of the more effective ways to help a person learn leadership is to ask him to observe a good leader and share with you afterwards what he learned. This way the mentee reaches independent conclusions. Observing and mentally processing the result helps the observer to own the lessons. I challenge my mentees to look for opportunities to mentor others, asking, "Who would you want to follow? The leader who is a good listener and willing to share, or the leader who is so self-absorbed, he fails to see opportunities to help those around him." It isn't necessary to ask or tell your mentee he is self-absorbed, and you don't have to point out their possible shortcomings. Let them observe and come to the conclusion.

It will help others perceive you as a leader if you are recommending or nominating others for awards, and promotions. Letting people know you think they are worthy can help them to grow. Once I learned I'd made the short list for company Fellow, I wrote out my Fellow's agenda. When I looked at it, I realized nothing on my list required me to be a Fellow in order to do accomplish the goals. In fact, the next year when I (falsely) assumed I had missed again, I arranged to change jobs and 'pretend' I was a company Fellow. At IBM, you get jobs after you are doing them, so I planned to do the job.

Mentoring relationships

I'm convinced the original apprentice/master relationship was a form of mentoring. The master got cheap labor in exchange for training the apprentice. The disappearance of this legal relationship has made finding mentors and being a mentor critical to training the next generation.

For many years, the only type of mentoring most people saw was the protégé/sponsor relationship. This one-on-one commitment often required the protégé to relinquish much freedom of action in exchange for a significant boost up the corporate ladder. Sometimes the intense commitment between sponsor and protégé can blind the sponsor to the weaknesses of the protégé. We all have weaknesses, but hopefully, we are striving to improve upon them and turn them into strengths. If the sponsor can't admit he picked a poor protégé, then the protégé may be promoted beyond his level of competence and the company suffers.

In my early years, I took for granted the natural exchange of information with my teammates and underestimated its mentoring value. This informal type of mentoring is, in my opinion, the most valuable. People are brought together by a mutual need to grow. Everyone learns from the interaction and everyone leaves satisfied. Remember, the best way to learn something is to teach it.

Despite the advantages of casual peer mentoring, you should seek to have formal mentors as well. Your peers may be just as confused about the cultural climate of your company as you are. Your peers may have little experience in managing their managers or their careers. You need advice from more experienced mentors for some things.

I once read a newspaper review about a mentoring book suggesting women should replace the 'sponsor/protégée' model with a more loosely coupled model having at least five mentors and in turn mentoring as least five mentees. This way, if the 'sponsor' leaves the work force, it is not a disaster for the protégée. With five mentees, poor choices are more readily obvious and easier to shed gently. With five mentors to choose from, one of them is likely to have the expertise you need on any given occasion.

Using this new model, I recommend one mentor should be of the opposite sex, one should be from outside the company (probably found through your professional organization), one should hold the next desired promotion, one should be at the same level, and one should be a new hire. If you are being mentored by this combination, you should also be mentoring a similar range of people. I recommend this model for everyone—male and female.

Observe your mentee in various settings

I have been mentoring a female PhD for a few years now. In my opinion, she is Fellow material, a brilliant inventor and clearly a leader.

Recently, she was proposed for a promotion. I was on the review board. A good friend of mine reviewed her references, receiving mixed signals. Many of her co-workers did not see her as an inventor. They indicated she was good at organizing other people's work, but rarely had an original idea. This was counter to my knowledge of her. I had been working with her one-on-one for several years and found her to be very creative. I couldn't understand how others would have such a different opinion of her. She did not get the promotion.

She asked me to do a mini-project with her. The project would be to brainstorm and submit invention disclosures in an area important to the company. Since it is an area I also think is important, we started weekly conference calls. After the first call, we invited another mentee to join us for the next call because we had moved into the area of his expertise.

As we reviewed for him the minutes of our previous meeting, her style changed. Instead of speaking with the confidence and certainty she displayed when she originally threw out her creative ideas, she sounded tentative as she reviewed them. She prefaced every one of her inventive ideas with "What if we could ...?"

I knew instantly why her reviews had been less than stellar. When working with a group, she flexed into her (female) facilitator mode, being inclusive and cooperative, offering suggestions (and very valid ones), but allowing others to take her ideas and run with them. She didn't take charge and demand acknowledgement for her contributions, but allowed others to believe they were the ones who came up with them. This will be an easy matter for her to correct, now she is aware of the problem, but I never would have seen it if we hadn't been working with a third party. When you mentor, you need to see your mentee in action—not only with yourself but also with others.

Handling sensitive information

As a mentor, you are likely to receive sensitive information from your mentee. With the exception of suicide plans, your job is to listen and not pass the information on to anyone. How can your mentee trust you if you promptly blab (gossip) about their concerns? It is a betrayal of their confidence. When you think a story will help someone else, ask if you may share it. Most people will allow you to share their experiences— although they may ask you to 'sanitize' things by disguising their identity—in order to help someone else. Ask your mentees to remind you when what they are sharing is not public information. The reminder will keep you from making mistakes.

What is the mentor's responsibility when a mentee confides they may leave the company? This is a delicate position. You feel a responsibility to your company to preserve its workforce, and you have a duty of confidentiality to your mentee. As one person put it, "It is the role of the mentor to always encourage the best choice for each person, the one that will provide challenge, growth potential, and better use of skills."

Advise your mentee to explore options within the company, unless you have reason to believe the mentee will be happier outside the organization, and offer to help them in their search. Ask permission to pass along word of their dissatisfaction to those who have the power to address their situation. Make use of your network on their behalf. It would be a shame for your corporation to miss the opportunity to retain skill by making appropriate adjustments. Of course, you may also have knowledge the mentee is about to be laid off or disciplined for some reason. You cannot pass along confidential information, but you can encourage your mentee to look elsewhere. In any case, advise your mentee to time their decision carefully.

Sometimes the problem is not quite as dramatic as leaving the company, but rather leaving the group. It still should be handled with care. If your mentee cannot trust you to keep their disclosures confidential, you are not doing your job as mentor.

A company will not thrive if the employees feel reluctant and trapped. Sometimes the answer is to find another job inside the same company. Sometimes it may be to leave. I encourage my mentees not to take their problems with them. If they learn to handle their problems where they are, then they are growing and will start at a different level if they change jobs inside or outside the company. If your mentee does not grow through and out of their problems, they will run into the same ones in their next job.

People are the same everywhere. According to a story I heard, a farmer is leaning against his fence when a car pulls up and stops next to him. The owner gets out and asks the farmer, "What are the people like in this town?" The farmer thinks a bit and then asks, "What are the people like where you live now?" The driver whines and complains, "They're horrible. I can't wait to leave them behind." The farmer comments, "You're going to find the people here are the same." So the driver moves on to the next town, looking for nice neighbors. Another car stops by the same farmer and its driver asks the same questions. The farmer responds the same way. This time the driver replies, "I have wonderful neighbors. I wouldn't think of moving except my job has moved." The farmer comments, "You're going to find people are the same here."

Not every problem is yours to fix

Some problems are not yours to fix, even if you are the mentor. Some people look to others to solve their problems. You can recognize them because they tend not to learn anything from previous sessions. Sometimes you wonder if they think because you are higher up in the organization than they are, that you have the power to make their problems vanish. If you do that, they won't grow and learn to solve their problems and move on to new ones. As a rule of thumb, try not to get involved. Go out of your way to drop comments about what a great job someone did on project X or to suggest, "You really should have John Doe show you the incredible research he has done." The mentor's job is to share his or her experience, not to solve the problem. Technical problems are an exception, but even then, decide whether the person just needs a little more time to solve it.

My manager in marketing would change the subject immediately if I started to whine or complain about things he could not be expected to fix. At first, it startled me because he was usually so polite. About the fourth time, I gained an appreciation that our conversations should stick to topics he could do something about.

It is not a mentor's job to solve problems, listen to whining, or settle minor disputes. It is a mentor's job to help the mentee grow and solve his or her own problems.

Mentoring is not managing

Your manager may also be your mentor, but be sure to keep the relationships separate. On occasion, when I need some mentoring from my manager, I request that he take off his management hat and put on his mentoring hat. This way he understands I'm not asking him to solve my problem or to take managerial action, but I am looking for mentoring advice. I've learned a lot from such advice. Often it provides me with the acceptable context in which I can communicate with another manager. His suggestions are usually an avenue I had not considered, but they feel like a good first step. Meanwhile, my manager is aware of my concern and will not be caught by surprise if my actions make waves. At least he knows what I intended to accomplish if I proceed to put my foot in my mouth.

Good mentors tell stories

Like good teachers, good mentors tell stories. Even if you're a new hire, with no work experience beyond flipping burgers during high school, you have stories to tell. Draw from your personal experience and the stories you have heard over the years to create examples for your mentees. Your past experience may hold the key to someone's greatest problem. Share with them. That's what mentoring is all about.

Managing People

At the Research Center, I somehow picked up the idea success that means being a manager. I can swear no one ever told me that. Still, I didn't question this assumption, so after a few years I began to feel like a failure because I wasn't a manager. Finally, I examined my assumptions. By my third year, I had seen enough to know the first-line management job was a bummer. You had responsibility without the corresponding resources or authority. It didn't take long to decide I wasn't interested. It wasn't until my second level manager told me, "Anyone who wants to be a manager and hasn't told their manager is stupid," that I realized becoming a manager is not an appointment from on high without participation from the employee. If you want to manage others, you have to let your manager know. You also need to explore the job requirements. Talk to your mentors. Find out if it's what you really want to do.

My thesis advisor finally showed me I was looking at management from the wrong perspective. He told me, "You don't want to be managed by the people who want to manage. It's like being on faculty committees. It's part of accepting your responsibilities and growing up." I'd been looking at what a manager's position would do for me, not what I could do with the position. The challenge of providing an environment where people can shine and do top-notch research appealed to me.

Months later, his words came back to me. Friends had invited me over to play games and tutor one of their children. I spent the whole time obsessed with the topic of being a manager. We discussed it from every possible angle and by Monday morning, I had decided I was ready and willing to become a manager.

The following week my manager asked, "How hard do we have to twist your arm to get you to accept being a manager?" Thanks to the advice I'd received months before, and the weekend spent considering the possibility, my response was, "Not at all. I'm willing to be a manager." As I left his office, I realized I didn't know what I had agreed to manage.

Managing others

Management is a service opportunity. Instead of being the sheep, you get to be the shepherd. You make sure your people have the resources they need to do their jobs. You interact with other teams and other departments to be sure your people are working on things that are important to the company. You make sure your people have the opportunity for training so they can advance in their careers. You get to help them solve some of their problems, and teach them how to solve others.

My first week as a manager was an interesting experience. One of my employees hit the roof. He was offended because I had been made his manager without his having any input. I tried everything, including trying to placate him. Do not follow my example. Trying to appease an employee when his objections are unreasonable is bad management.

I assumed a manager's job was to hire great people, spend the budgeted money wisely, set directions, and help transfer research into products that make money. The reality was rather different. The first-line manager's job frequently has no official hiring slots for those great people, and often no budget.

As a manager, your job is to maintain open lines of communication. I found it helped to summarize critical meetings in writing, including any expected deliverables. Then if I had understood wrong, my error was uncovered in the first twenty-four hours and not after a project failed.

One cardinal rule I have for dealing with both management and employees is, 'no surprises'. It's the same rule my first manager used with me. If an employee is doing poorly, they should not be surprised to receive a poor rating at the end of the year. Similarly, an employee should not go over his or her manager's head without first trying to resolve the issue with the manager. In very hierarchical cultures going over your manager's head may constitute treason. The 'no surprises' rule holds good in many aspects of life, such as church work and dealing with neighbors.

The greatest compliment you can pay your employees is to use what they create. Create an environment where people can grow and they will pay you back by blossoming and growing. The other side of the coin is equally true; the greatest compliment your employees can pay you is to create/perform outstandingly. When they do so, you know you have done your job.

Leadership is a management skill

Leadership takes practice, and leadership is necessary in managing people. You can move up your professional organization's ladder and learn critical skills in advance of when you will need them in your own corporation. Volunteer organizations are also an excellent place to learn how to take charge and provide direction. I know people who became leaders out of self-defense. They found the chaos resulting from everyone hoping someone else will take charge to be painful. They preferred to organize an outing rather than live through the confusion. It takes less time to organize than to wait for someone else to organize, and of course, you enjoy outings more if you are able to include things you want to do.

Handling difficult people requires first recognizing they are difficult because it works for them. As a manager, and as a human being, try to determine why the individual is difficult. What makes it work for them? Do they need attention? Do they have valid objections to the chosen path, but they express their objections poorly? Are they afraid? Try to get to the reasons, in your own mind. Then take back control of your happiness.

Learning to take control of your happiness around people who seem determined to spoil it takes practice, but is much easier once you realize you have the choice to give them the power to make you unhappy or not. Remind yourself that you are least tolerant of your own faults in others. You are more tolerant of faults you don't express. Examine your behavior and try not to blame the difficult person you are dealing with.

A cousin recommended *Coping with Difficult People* to me. She had heard about it when she was dealing with someone who was hard to help. While you are learning to handle someone difficult, be sure to take a good look at yourself. Do other people find you difficult? I was surprised to recognize myself in the book as the engineer who talks louder and tells you more, if you don't agree or understand his position. *The Gentle Art of Verbal Self-Defense* is helpful when you are dealing with abusive individuals. There are other books on the market worth checking out from the library.

Situational leadership as a management style

When I first heard the words 'situational leadership', I thought, "Oh no, leadership with no principles." I was wrong. 'Situational' does not refer to circumstances, but to the skill and willingness of the employee. Your management style changes as employees grow and change. One style does not fit all. In fact, what is good for a beginner is bad for an expert and vice versa.

Hersey and Blanchard's book *Management of Organizational Behavior* was an eye-opener for me. I thought more time with employees was always good. Hersey and Blanchard have a chart divided into four quadrants. The bottom axis is emphasis on the task. The side axis is the interaction-time spent with people. A bell shaped curve starts in the bottom right quadrant, moves up to the top right quadrant, across to the top left quadrant, and down to the bottom left quadrant.

Quadrant One, on the bottom right, represents managing beginners; people who don't have necessary skills. It is labeled "Telling". The amount of time spent with these employees is minimized. Give them just enough that they can learn to do their job. Anything more is counterproductive and can be overwhelming. 'Time spent' is a reward, and to reward the beginner with time may de-motivate them from moving along the curve and mastering the needed skills. However, the extreme where the curve begins is labeled "Yelling". Try to avoid it. Have enough respect for your employees to allow them to keep their dignity.

Quadrant Two (top right) represents managing employees who have the skill to do the mechanics of the job, but need to develop good judgment. Hersey and Blanchard call this "Selling." Now that they can do the job, your employees need to understand the 'whys and wherefores'. Having frequent lunches with them is quite appropriate. This is also the time to share 'tricks of the trade'. Shortcuts and other time savers will be appreciated. Those same shortcuts, if introduced earlier, could mean the task is never properly learned.

Once the employee has developed good judgment, do not abandon them. They still need feedback, but no longer as a coach. Start weaning them from the assumption their job is simply to execute someone else's plans. They are now ready to develop the plans. Allow them to participate in the process of generating a plan of action. The interaction-time stays high while concern for the task drops. Quadrant Three is "Participating."

When someone is well trained and demonstrates good judgment, it is time to delegate. This is Quadrant Four. Interaction-time drops drastically, otherwise the temptation to micromanage may become too much to resist. You can interact in other ways, but being too nosy about the details of their job sends signals of, "I don't trust you with the job." The extreme of delegating, out where the bell-curve hits the origin, is labeled "Neglect." Not a good place to be.

When things are going well, the book recommends moving along the curve ahead of your employee. This gives them room to grow. Don't take too big a jump or they will be confused by the change in behavior. I have found it useful to go through this model of management with my employees and to reach mutual agreement on where the person believes they are and how they want to be treated. Later, a gentle hint from the employee that they want to move toward the next quadrant keeps me from developing bad habits.

The book recommends never moving more than one quadrant along the curve at time. A jump backwards from "delegate" to "telling" when things are going badly is not appropriate. Instead, back up to "Participating". As the book says, "When an employee is having trouble, get behind them on the curve and push. Don't just allow them to go into free fall and fail."

I vividly remember hearing the description of situational management on a Wednesday during a week-long Research Management Training session. That evening I checked in on an employee who operated in the "delegate" quadrant and heard myself treat him two quadrants away in "selling" mode. I suggested he make a certain phone call, and then went into the details of what he should say. I stopped in mid-sentence and said, "I'm sure you know how to handle the call, get back to me if you have any questions," and walked out. Finally, a solution to overwork—quit bugging employees who are well trained and ready to spread their wings. Give them the freedom to soar alone.

Take management training courses whenever they are available to you. They are a part of growing into your next level of competence. Don't depend on the few brief things mentioned here to make a manager of you. You wouldn't skip Quantum Mechanics because a friend gave you a synopsis. Get a copy of Hersey and Blanchard's book, either from the book store or from the library, and read it before you begin your management duties. You haven't learned everything they have to say from reading these few paragraphs.

The significance of expectations

Playing to a person's strengths and bringing out the best is dependent upon your expectations and perceptions of that person. We've all heard stories about the impact of the teacher's expectations on students. I remember reading about a seventh-grade teacher who was thrilled to discover her classes were filled with geniuses. Their IQ scores were in the 130s and above. At the end of the year, the principal praised her for the great class results. She said, "With IQs like that, what else could I expect?" The principal responded, "But they've never been tested." "I found their IQ scores on my desk the opening day of school," exclaimed the teacher. "Those were their locker numbers," the principal explained.

When I was a TA, one student puzzled me. He always got the hardest quiz problem right, often the only student in class who did, and yet he usually flunked the rest of the test. Fortunately, he came to my office so we could talk. He suffered from test anxiety. On the hardest problem, he relaxed and enjoyed solving it, but he expected to fail the test, so he usually did. After some drill, it was obvious he knew the material, so we talked about test taking, and after a few sessions, he changed his expectations. After that, he became a straight A student.

What we think about a person may be more important than what we say or do. When I went to Germany after high school, it only took six weeks for me to believe I was dumb. I was convinced I was the first American failure abroad. Then my parents visited and we traveled together for three weeks. They only cared that my German got us a room for the night. Suddenly, I was brilliant. I regained my confidence and had a marvelous time. Expect the best from the people around you, and they will give it to you.

Be ready to forgive mistakes

We don't live in a perfect world. If you can't forgive the mistakes of others, your life will be miserable. People make mistakes, even when they act with good intentions. If you can't forgive yourself for mistakes, you will live with them your entire life.

Catherine Marshall's book, *Something More* made a deep impression on me. Catherine told of a friend's rebellious daughter finally asking forgiveness when her parents gave up their "oughts" against her. I had already begun to conclude what we think about others may have a bigger influence on their lives than even what we say.

Advanced Degrees

Is a PhD worth it?

When I'm mentoring, and someone asks for advice about getting a PhD, I tell them, "You should get a PhD only if you can't not get it. A doctorate should be a passion and internally driven." Studies have shown the pay lost during those years is unlikely ever to be recouped. Also, a PhD will price you out of some entry level positions. However, a PhD is generally required for entry level jobs at research institutions. Your PhD years constitute a low-paying job in which you are allowed to research where your heart takes you.

A Master's degree is another thing. Generally, your Master's will not price you out of entry level jobs. Many people get their Master's after working for several years. By then they knew their specialty and want the formal recognition and the extra systematic studies. Many Master's programs consist mostly of course work. More and more, the Master's is necessary for credibility, and to reach the top pay scales.

If you have not yet completed your Bachelor's degree, the answer is obvious. You can definitely improve your position by completing your education. I know two technicians who elevated themselves into the engineering ranks by completing their undergraduate educations in engineering. It took them seven years of night school while they worked full time to support their families. Even with a degree, promotion is not automatic, but the degree helps your manager show a promotion is merited. Many companies have a tuition refund program for completed coursework.

Towards the end of 2003, I became convinced technical people need to move up the value chain by completing technical degrees.

I also believe schools of higher education need to recognize that returning professionals are not children. When they bring their own money, rules should be easy to bend. Relaxing restrictions will help us move talented people, laid-off workers, and even retirees up the value chain.

Not everyone desiring to return to school fits into the same situation. Early in 2004, I wrote down some different categories:

1) Full-time working professionals with corporate sponsorship may have business interrupt their ability to be on campus.

2) Unemployed professionals (possibly recently laid-off) may be able to attend full-time and be on campus as needed.

3) Retirees switching fields to pursue their passion, possibly in a different field— able to be on campus as needed.

I also considered the university barriers I believed needed altering. Some of the ones I hoped universities would reconsider were:

1) Taking GREs (cost, time, pressure)—Waive.

2) January application for starting in the fall—Allow professionals to enter at any time.

3) Must complete Master's and PhD within six years from start of Master's—waive.

4) Class attendance—allow maximum flexibility if material is mastered—e.g. take quizzes ahead of schedule if a business trip is scheduled.

No one should go back to school without carefully considering the costs—the financial costs, the time, and the emotional commitment. I think the verses from Luke 14:28-30 apply, "For which of you, intending to build a tower, sitteth not down first, and counteth the cost, whether he have sufficient to finish it? Lest haply, after he hath laid the foundation, and is not able to finish it, all that behold it begin to mock him, Saying, This man began to build, and was not able to finish." Returning to school is a serious decision requiring serious consideration.

A professor from a nearby university was looking for more industry/university interaction. I shared with him my conviction that industry and higher education need to cooperate to 'move people up the value chain'. He invited me to their educational advisory committee meeting the next month. They promptly appointed me co-chair of a task force to explore defining both the problem and various approaches to the solution. Apparently, they had already been asking similar questions and were glad to be able to hear the industrial perspective.

Together, we worked out a way to relax some of the admission requirements for professionals returning to school for advanced degrees. Your local university is just as likely to work with you to relax some of their requirements. Find your thesis advisor. Find your thesis topic. Work with your employer and your local university to make it happen. Universities all over the country are aware of the needs of working professionals who are also part-time students, and a movement is growing to accommodate them.

Find your thesis advisor before applying

At IBM Boulder, our first step is a pilot program. Professors from various departments agreed to give technical talks about their research, and stay for a roundtable discussion. The professors are interested in meeting potential students and can direct students to other professors if the interests make a better match.

Since admissions approval comes at the department level, having a professor as an advocate makes it easier to tailor requirements to individual situations. Some students may receive credit for work experience. Distance learning classes in one department can often be applied towards the requirements of another department.

I call this the 'magic'. If you find a thesis advisor with a passion in the area of your passion, and you have determined that your company needs research in this area, your thesis isn't a solution looking for a problem, but the search for a solution to a problem. The likelihood of your company paying tuition and allowing you to work at least part time on your research is much higher if you discuss the connection with your management before you apply.

Don't believe everything you read

I'm including a brief e-mail I received to illustrate the issues you may encounter.

```
Subject: Department A or B …

I've investigated the choices and
Department  A appears to be the best
option.
Department B has a requirement in their
handbook stating the PhD  candidate must
complete 9 hours on campus in each of 2
```

```
consecutive semesters.  This is untenable
for me.  They are  asking me to be a full
time college student for two semesters to
get started and  that's unacceptable.
Department A on the other hand does not
have the on-campus requirement. Further,
they have an on-line Master's program that
might facilitate with the completion of
course work for the breadth  requirement.
After reading through the degree
requirements for both Department A and B I
came away thinking the Department A program
had fewer "hoops" than the Department B
program.
thanks
```

This person's future thesis advisor happened to have a joint appointment with departments A and B. He did not know this difference existed between requirements. According to him, 'on campus' means what the advisor says it means. He recommended Department B and the student enrolled.

This is not the first time a student reading an official university website found discouraging information. In this case, the student believed she would have to repeat her Master's degree course work. My reaction as her de facto advisor was, "No way. You can take new classes whose contents are important for your thesis and your future work, but not old classes unless they are shown to be useful." Her official thesis advisor agreed with me. She made the mistake of asking the official record keeper and was told she definitely had to repeat the work. Only after being notified (two useful courses later) to form her thesis committee did she truly believe the redundant work could be avoided.

Beware of university patent rules

In the fall of 2001, I taught a semester course at a nearby university. While signing the paperwork to become a Visiting Professor, I discovered they expected me to sign a statement keeping all intellectual property (IP) rights between the university and me. Since IBM is the sole owner of my IP, including inventions created outside of working hours, I didn't have the right to sign that statement. IP rules vary between universities, but you must check. As an employee, you probably do not have the right to assign IP rights to the university.

Inquire about the university's patent policy before you apply. Some universities have become greedy and won't negotiate. If you have effectively lined up your thesis with your day job, you expect to invent. Your employer expects to benefit from your invention.

Confidential Disclosure Agreement

You must have your thesis advisor sign a confidential disclosure agreement (CDA). Part of the magic of lining up your day job and your thesis is to work on a problem which is important (and potentially profitable) to your company. If it has business value, your company will be interested in patenting it. Without a CDA, if your advisor is not a co-inventor, talking about your thesis with him or her instantly starts the one-year clock ticking in the US and loses all foreign patent rights.

Getting started

If you want an advanced degree, find out if your company supports you. Will they reimburse tuition? Will they allow you a flexible working schedule? If your passion is research, are you working on something that would make a good thesis topic? Will your new degree benefit the company?

Next, check with the local university to see if they will support you. Are their admissions guidelines flexible? Will they allow you to miss class as required? Can you waive time limits? What is their IP rule? Is there a professor with whom you share a passion?

Finally, talk it over with your mentors. Can they smooth the way for you in relaxing university rules? Will one of them act as de facto advisor for you?

If you are an experienced professional, well-known outside your own company, take the initiative to enable others to move up the value chain by obtaining advanced degrees. Work with your local university to relax admissions guidelines for returning professionals. Make sure your company has an education policy. Seek out the best and brightest in your company and give them a leg up. As a mentor, your job is growing the next generation.

Moving Professionals up the Value Chain

Growing mentees through Mini-Projects

In 2003, I proved multiple mini-projects are an effective way to leverage my time and talents while growing top technical talent in my division. Encouraging my mentee to take ownership and drive the project while consulting with me allows me to be involved without being consumed. I combine growing the next generation with staying technically active. Those working on mini-projects with me have the right to use ten to fifteen percent of their time to pursue their project. Since most of them still perform their regular jobs, the net effect may be overtime, but at least they get to have fun. I must agree their project is important to the company, and my mentee must be passionate about the project. Instead of talking about how to succeed, I get to help them be successful.

In May 2004, I found a clipping I'd saved from the October 11, 1995 *The Christian Science Monitor* (p.4) titled "Nobel Prizes: Why US dominates—so far". The article claims 50% of Nobel Prize winners worked for or with another Nobel Prize winner. After re-reading the article, I made sure people were officially 'working with a Fellow' (me) and made our mini-projects more visible.

I frequently wonder how many Fellows worked for or with another Fellow earlier in their career. I know of five, which is about nine percent. As my manager pointed out, the management track automatically guarantees a manager will work for the next management level. That doesn't necessarily happen on the technical track. He worked for a Fellow his first years in the company and appreciates the fact I have both early and late tenure engineers and developers working with me.

At the end of 2004 I wrote, "My project to encourage universities to lower their barriers for full-time working professionals getting advanced degrees is progressing. Several mini-project collaborators are engaged in advanced degrees while working full time and I am learning from their experiences."

Light a fire under your mentees

One of the first software developers I encouraged to go for an advanced degree is working on her PhD thesis in the Math Department at a nearby University. Several years ago, I grew tired of hearing that she had made a mistake when she chose to complete a second Master's in order to leave school with her husband rather than finish a PhD. One day in the halls, I turned to her and said, "Either go get your PhD or shut up. I don't care which, but I don't want to hear that again." I'm not any better than Mom was at tolerating whining.

One of the senior engineers was a bit more practical about the whole process. He arranged to have me invited to give a talk at his Alma Mater. My mentee accompanied us, and he introduced her to the math department. I knew she had been accepted into the program before I wrote her recommendation. Since she was switching fields, she took classes for a few years and then passed the qualifying exam (a few months before her first child was born) with flying colors. She and her thesis advisor have submitted a joint invention disclosure, she is now working on her proposal, and she expects to graduate soon.

Another of my mentees took a longer road to advancement. Five years before I met her, she started a computer science Master's degree program while seven months pregnant with her first child. She finished the program after her third child was born. We became acquainted when, in the fall of 2002, she asked me to teach her oldest son to swim. Instead, I taught him to float since, once he was not afraid of water, he could learn to swim in regular swimming classes. Periodically, we met at the YMCA. As her three children played in the wading pool, she asked questions about my research. She started helping me outside of regular hours and this eventually led to her working for me part-time in 2003. Late that year, we realized our mini-project included a potential PhD thesis.

In December 2003, the two of us, plus another mentor, invited her favorite local professor to lunch on site. About fifteen minutes into lunch, he leaned back and said, "OK, I'd like to know what you want from me." I answered, "I want to be her de facto thesis advisor, and you to be her official advisor. I'll handle the day-to-day training if you can give her a half hour every two months to answer questions." When he responded, "I can probably do better than that," I knew she was in. I'm glad I didn't know the acceptance statistics (about 1 in 17) until after she was officially admitted.

In January 2004, she applied to his university for the PhD program in Computer Science. Our first meeting with her official thesis advisor at the university occurred before she knew she had been accepted. Her advisor said this was the first time he had ever discussed possible thesis proposals before a candidate had even been admitted. She started her course work by taking a Spring-semester class while still awaiting the admission decision. She took another class in the fall, which completed her course work. She received permission to enroll in independent thesis research after only six units of classes. She completed her PhD qualifying exams in 2005, her thesis proposal in 2006, and hopes to be done in 2007.

Another Software Developer finished his Executive MBA from a local university in May 2004. He has always had a passion for market intelligence and trying to read between the lines. He has been happy to apply his skills to figuring out how to grow our business profitably.

Since the departments control admissions, you can sometimes circumvent the system. A different Software Developer started a new mini-project with me in 2004. We had an invention disclosure submitted within a few weeks. He was already taking one class before he decided to apply to the PhD program. By then we knew the value of finding a thesis advisor before applying, so before he submitted his application, he asked his professor to be his advisor. His advisor then told the department admissions person (according to hearsay), "This is my graduate student. Get him in."

One Software Engineer was already a PhD candidate at a local university in the ECEE department when I started mentoring him in 2004. Our mini-project was to introduce him to the broader company (networking) and help him recognize the immediate value of his initial results. Within a month of starting our mini-project, his thesis advisor was under a CDA and a patent application was in the works. The patent was filed before his paper was submitted. I am proud to say he passed his comprehensive examination and expects to finish in 2007. He presented his first conference paper in 2005 in Germany, and submitted another on his thesis topic. I continue to encourage him to network throughout the company so his breakthroughs can be incorporated into company tools.

The previous examples demonstrate magic. A little effort on the part of the mentor, and a lot of effort on the part of the mentee, resulted in phenomenal change. In every company throughout the world, there are people of talent wasting away for want of that little bit of effort on the part of the mentor. Those people are willing to do their part, but they need help. Your job, as a mentor, is to help move them up the value chain so they can help to change the world.

Summary

- Give back by mentoring now
- Helping others thrive helps you
- Never stop learning—consider the next degree
- Find your passion (and thesis advisor) before applying to graduate school.

6

Creativity and Inventing

*A*nyone can be an inventor. The key to a successful invention is identifying a problem. You've probably already invented many times in your life. If what you created solved your problem, is there a chance it might solve someone else's similar problem?

My oldest nephew's wife is a stay-at-home mom with two small girls. About the time her youngest daughter graduated to a sippy cup, the eldest announced she was too old for such things. "Sippy cups are for babies." She wanted to move up to juice boxes. Juice boxes are a wonderful packaging invention, but they have one problem. When you jab the straw into the box (or pouch), you squeeze, and the juice flies out the straw and all over you.

My nephew's wife looked around for a solution to the problem, but she didn't find one. There are holders on the market for juice boxes, but they only fit one size box and they don't fit the cup-holders in cars and strollers. Eventually she found a couple of examples that would fit all sizes and also fit into cup-holders, but they were too large for her daughters to handle, and too ugly (black and gray) for them to want. Her solution was marvelously simple and the patent is pending for her No-Squeeze juice box holder.

If a good solution had been available, she wouldn't have had a problem. Instead, she took her make-shift solution, refined it, and now has a marketable product.

Too often, research ends up with solutions looking for problems. If you identify a novel solution, you need to ask a second question, "Will anyone pay for it?" Does your widget solve someone else's problem? Can you have it manufactured in volume for a cost that allows you to sell at a profit? If you want to be able to file overseas, you have to keep your solution confidential. If you talk about it, you have to file in the US within a year and forget about foreign filings.

There are commercial and public websites with patent databases. The United States Patent and Trademark Office website is at http://www.uspto.gov/. The Delphion website is another example at http://www.delphion.com/. You can read and browse patents there, but only have to provide a credit card number if you want a printed copy of the patent.

The story of my wet suit patent is a long story, but it will show you part of what's involved. Your cost will be higher than you thought, and the process will take longer than you expected. In the end, you may have nothing. Or you may hit a grand-slam.

When people hear I have over seventy issued patents, they often ask, "Don't you wish you owned them personally?" Through the years, I may have wondered a bit, but now I know the answer is definitely no. Only about one percent of patents earn back their costs. The fees for issued patents are due every few years. The fees grow higher over time. I'm grateful I don't have to maintain them.

My Wet Suit Patent

What is Intellectual Property?

Intellectual Property (IP) is much more than just patents. Patents only apply to inventions. IP can be a trademark—how a product or service is identified. Copyrights for works of authorship are IP. A trade secret is something I know and you don't know and is included in a company's IP. A fairly recent best seller, titled *Rembrandts in the Attic*, encourages companies to recognize that their IP may have hidden value worth systematically searching out.

The United States Constitution provides, "Congress shall have Power ... To promote the progress of Science and useful Arts, by securing for limited Times to Authors and Inventors the exclusive Right to their respective Writings and Discoveries;" (Sect. 8, paragraph 8). Congress in turn provides, "Whoever invents or discovers any new and useful process, machine, manufacture, or composition of matter, or any new and useful improvement thereof, may obtain a patent therefore, subject to the conditions and requirements of this title." (35 USC 101)

My first day on the job, I assigned my IP rights to IBM. This was considered a reasonable trade 30-some years ago, because most people stayed with one company their entire working career. As a lawyer's daughter, I appreciated the company HR person carefully explaining so I understood what I was signing. At that time, I had the opportunity to exclude any previously created IP. I didn't think the widget I designed and built for my thesis experiments counted as IP. It was novel, but had no business value. I wrote in 'none'.

At IBM, if an invention does not relate to current or future company business, you can submit an invention disclosure and ask for the rights back. Let me emphasize, this is extremely rare. More than a decade ago, a colleague, and another company employee had invented a bicycle with a continuously recharging battery. They built a working prototype. After many years, they were within a few months of their hoped for patent. They had successfully responded to the patent examiner's questions and issues. Then another patent—filed earlier and covering their invention—issued and the examiner rejected their application.

Background for the wet suit invention

One of the requirements for Rescue Diver Certification is to assist in several open-water scuba diving classes. Carter Lake (about a half-hour north of Longmont) is frequently used for local classes. On a Saturday in September 2000, I arrived at the lake. The dive shop loaned me farmer johns and a shortie and hood. I brought my own environmental suit, gloves, buoyancy control device (BCD), regulator, and booties. Normally, I only wore the environmental suit, but Carter Lake is cold.

The lake was low and we had to suit up on the rocks below and to the right of the boat ramp. With considerable struggle, I managed to suit up except for my fins. I walked into the lake and promptly lost my balance, falling backwards in about two feet of water. There I was, floating on the water like an over-turned turtle. Normally, I would simply roll over and put my feet down, but I couldn't move my arms and legs and knew if I rolled over, I would drown. The farmer johns and shortie combined were so stiff I was helpless. Fortunately, someone was there to help. Back on shore, I removed the shortie. Later I realized I had on a scuba tank and could have put the regulator in my mouth for air, so I wouldn't have drowned. Hindsight is wonderful. I still wore my environmental suit under the farmer johns. At least I could move my arms freely, although breathing was difficult. By now I'd missed all the prep work I'd come early to help with.

Four big balls floated on the surface, and about twenty feet below them and attached by lines, four pipes made a large square—the dive platform. A canvas tarp attached to the pipes formed the actual platform where the instructor lay. The students followed the lines from the balls to the platform, and hung onto the pipes. The water is 58 degrees at 20 feet below the surface, and so murky you can barely see the student to the right, but you can't see the face of his buddy. Since I was supposed to make sure both were okay, I signaled the question "OK?" to the far away student, watched the hand of the student next to me as he signaled back "OK", and then guessed all was well.

Even with both farmer johns and a shortie, the thinner students were shivering by the end of their dives. I thought I was fine because I didn't get cold until toward the end of the third dive. But it took me half an hour to make the trip when I snorkeled to shore for a rest and to pick up the last pair of students. Since I was used to snorkeling 32 laps of the pool several times a week, you can understand this was unusual. I felt like all my muscles were about to cramp.

My schedule that morning included four dives. I hated opting out of the last dive and leaving them short of assistants, but I felt it wasn't safe for me to dive again. I got out of the wet suit and could finally breathe again. Then I drank more than a gallon of water while I waited for the last dive to finish. Later, I learned drinking that much water in an hour isn't a good idea, and the bruises on my shoulders from the farmer johns made me realize the rule of "if you can get into a wet suit, it's the right size" doesn't work with the environmental suit to help the wet suit slip on. The bruises lasted two weeks.

The Ah Ha Moment

After helping the group pack up, I drove home vowing never to wear a wet suit again. However, wet suits are essential in Carter Lake. Then I thought, "There has to be a better, more comfortable, safer, wet suit." I started playing mentally with the idea of a safer suit. My thoughts wandered along the lines of: "What if—the wet suit didn't change volume? Then its thermal properties wouldn't change. It could be thinner, because its thermal protection wouldn't be reduced to 20% at 130 feet. It would be safer, because I'd need less weight to compensate." I packed thirty pounds of weight for the shortie and farmer johns, eighteen pounds for the farmer johns alone, and without a wet suit, I only used six pounds of lead. If the volume didn't change with depth, less skill would be necessary.

There are three major ways to lose heat:
1) Heat loss from radiation—not a problem in scuba,
2) Conduction—a major problem in diving because the thermal conductivity of water is 20 times that of air, and
3) Convection currents—a significant problem because hot water rises and acts like a circulation pump to pull cold water into the suit.

Neoprene gets its insulating power from air bubbles. When the water pressure below the surface squeezes the air bubbles, they reduce in size and much of the thermal protection is lost. A diver is in greater danger of heat-stroke on the surface than he is of having a diving accident below water. The sport would be safer if wet suits were cooler in the boat or when walking to the entry point.

The first idea I had was to use hollow beads to provide the insulating properties. Then volume is unlikely to change in the one to five atmospheric pressures found under water during recreational diving. I also wondered about a gel—form-fitting to stop water currents—but not rigid. I thought about packaging beads in fabric, quilt-like.

Wrote up invention disclosure

Three weeks later, I came into the office on a Saturday and wrote the invention disclosure. In the last section, I asked for the rights back. I wrote, "Since I am assuming the company is not interested in being in the wet suit business, I am requesting the rights to the idea of a wet suit with neutral buoyancy be returned so I can develop it with non-company scuba experts."

About a month later, I expanded the invention disclosure. I added outdoor clothing. In the case of clothing, positive buoyancy for floating could provide added safety. This time I wrote, "I am asking for the rights to clothing (excluding wearable computer-related items which are the company's business) and cloth/materials useful for insulating people from the environment."

A few weeks later, I did a patent search. I wondered if someone else had already invented my suit. If so, I could forget about it. I searched for "wet suit", "wet suite", "scuba", "microspheres", references to relevant patents, and everything else I could think of. In the end, I printed fewer than twenty patents out of the thousands of abstracts I looked at.

About two weeks later, I was notified the rights would be assigned to me. The assignment letter arrived a few weeks later.

Then I realized I needed a confidential disclosure before I talked to anyone, including relatives and potential implementers.

A few days before the New Year, I contacted a Virginia patent attorney I knew had filed patents in the area, and in January, I provided him with a detailed embodiment including an evaluation of those 20 patents.

Patent filed

Months later the final draft was faxed to me. It was outstanding, needing only a few typos and one concept corrected. When you work with draft patents, correct incorrect concepts with the wording for the correct concept. That way your attorney will understand what you're getting at. The patent application was filed on June 11, 2001. The filed application arrived with an invoice enclosed.

The first office action arrived six months later. At work, I sometimes deal with office actions from patents filed five years previously. This was unusually quick. Apparently, there weren't many wet suit patent applications in the Patent Office. The attorney asked for my comments. He was pleased the cited patents had already expired. This meant they could not block me from implementing the invention. I went to the local library, looked up some data, and sent it to him. The attorney responded three months later by amending the independent claims and giving some arguments. A copy of the office action arrived with the invoice enclosed.

Three months later, we received a second and final office action. Again, the attorney asked for comments. The new office action cited additional expired patents. I answered with a nine page evaluation. The attorney responded two months later by adding, "having a given interstitial volume when packed together" to independent claims, plus some arguments for the examiner. I received a copy of this with the invoice enclosed.

A year after the US filing, I needed to file overseas. Since I hadn't decided which countries to include, my attorney filed the application with a fee to buy time. This gave us another eighteen months before we had to determine specific nations. Again, the copy arrived with an invoice enclosed.

By now, I realized I should have asked for the cost to issue instead of an estimate of the costs to file. The costs differ by a factor of about two.

The examiner responded to the last office action, "The most recent amendment does not place the case in condition for allowance and applicant's arguments are not persuasive. More specifically, examiners response to arguments in the most recent office action remain as stated." The attorney explained I had some choices: 1) I could give up, 2) I could immediately appeal, but he did not advise this because there was a four year backlog in the appeals process, 3) I could accept a split because a few of the claims had been allowed. We could file a continuation in part (CIP) to start the process over on the remaining claims. I would pay two sets of fees for the lifetime of the patents, or 4) I could request a continued examination (RCE).

We filed the RCE with most of the previous amendments removed. This time we added to the independent claims, "said rigid wall being of a thickness to provide approximately neutral buoyancy and to maintain constant volume to a pressure corresponding to a depth of at least 130 feet in water." A copy of the RCE arrived with the invoice for the additional patent office fees, extra claims, and the attorney's fees.

Less than a month later, the attorney left a message on my home phone to call him the next day—a Saturday. His office answered and said he wasn't in, but I could leave him a message. About five minutes later my phone rang, and the attorney announced, "The patent has been allowed." He had to repeat it before I understood what he meant, and then I yelled. He said he didn't want to miss my reaction.

Soon, an invoice arrived. I could prepay the "small entity issue fee" (half the large enterprise fee), the publication fee, and the attorney's fees. US Patent 6,519,774 "Scuba Wet Suit With Constant Buoyancy," issued February 18, 2003.

Foreign filings

In December 2002, the eighteen months from date of filing was up. I was no better prepared to select additional nations for filing than I had been at the beginning. I could buy another years' extension by filing with the World IP Organization. The US application was published in December, even though we knew it would issue in a few months. I received a copy of the World IP filing with enclosed invoice.

In February, I received a phone message from a trade show suggesting I buy space to show off my wet suit. Several mail solicitations came from companies who offered to market my invention or to sell my patent. I was leery because I've read articles about fly-by-night companies and inventors losing their invention without fair remuneration.

My assumed time-scale had been four years to issue—not less than two years. I was not prepared to go forward yet.

When I explored which nations to file in, I asked the right questions. I asked for an estimate of the costs to get the patent issued rather than to get the application filed. The answers were more than I was willing to pay. So in December 2003, I let the deadline pass for foreign filings. I had assumed I could cover the world for about twice the US filing costs. My budget had been blown getting the US patent issued. Dealing with the rest of the world was more than ten times more expensive. The final decision came easily when I asked myself, "Joan, will you be willing to go to court in these other countries to sue for infringement?" The answer was a strong, "No."

Being a Fellow kept me busy, so there was little time left over for independent research. Finally, I hired someone to research the thermal properties of microspheres in neoprene. He worked diligently until he unexpectedly got a job with a start-up that needed his talents. Our research has been on hold.

Finding Your Inventing Style

Why do some people get lucky and always seem to be on good projects while others miss the golden opportunities? The following stories give tips on picking research topics, technical problem solving, and handling the sabotaging fears of success and failure.

I was hired directly out of graduate school as a Research Staff Member (RSM) in the Exploratory Printing Technologies Group in the Applied Research Department at the T.J. Watson Research Center. My assignment was to invent new ways to leave marks on paper. This included everything except ink jet printing. In my first weeks, I was given some excellent advice, "Don't rush into the lab, because the first problem you find is unlikely to be the most important." I would also suggest you temporarily apprentice yourself to someone more experienced in order to learn the ropes.

My manager had a favorite saying, "You can always invent your way out of a trap." This meant if you felt trapped, you could invent or find more important work and request you be allowed to work on it instead. Early in my career, I decided to test the theory. I attended a presentation on data compression. I hadn't known about the presentation in advance, but my co-workers asked me why I was heading the wrong direction in the halls, so I turned around and joined them. I walked out convinced I had the answer to a problem mentioned by the presenter. On Saturday mornings, I frequently found myself with a ruler looking at magazines and muttering to myself, "It ought to work. It ought to work." That presentation, and the ideas that came out of it, sent me into the field of data compression.

My personal style

Friends ask me, "How do you come up with your inventions?" My answer tends to be, "I'm trying to solve real problems." Most of my inventions are in response to hearing about a need. Sometimes I've consciously used tricks I learned in Dr. George Polya's Stanford Frosh Seminar on "How to solve it, or what to do when you don't know what to do."

One of the techniques I learned from his brain-teaser problems is that sometimes the simplest approach is brute force. His example had something to do with the age of twins who had a younger brother. If you wrote down all combinations (less than 30), there was only one set of three ages with the duplicate numbers larger than the third number.

When I want to write fast code, I start with brute force code. This allows me to confirm that I understand the problem. Then, solutions that are more elegant will pop into my mind in the middle of the night or early morning. The process may take several iterations. When I can draw a simple flow chart of the solution, I know I have found simplicity with elegance

Start with a real problem. Juice boxes squirt juice when you squeeze them. Children squeeze juice boxes. Look at all possible solutions until you locate the one best solution. When you find the solution that works—you don't get juice on your shirt—you have solved the problem. Your next step is to refine the solution. In the case of the juice box holder, find the proper colors and the right size for the user. Small children usually prefer bright primary colors to black and grey, and they have small hands. Continue refining until you have an easy, simple, elegant solution.

My second day on the job led to my first invention. My manager was suggesting areas of possible research. He talked about ultrasonic printing, but didn't know how to get the wavelength down to printing dimensions. He came from an optics background where light is the focus. From his perspective, light came as transverse waves—the waves rippling perpendicular to the direction of travel. When I was a TA, I attended a lecture on waves. The professor demonstrated both transverse and longitudinal waves. I can still picture his demonstrations with a slinky hanging from the ceiling. For transverse waves, he took the loose end and swung it side to side. The slinky responded with waves that moved pieces of it from side to side, as they traveled up and down the slinky. Then he demonstrated longitudinal waves. He moved the loose end up and down. The waves compressed and decompressed up and down the slinky until they damped out completely.

As my manager explained the problems with ultrasonics waves, I mentally replayed and rehearsed demonstrations from that lecture five years before, becoming more and more puzzled. I asked him what the problem with the resolution was. I remembered the wave lecture and the example from Western films of the train robbers listening for the train by putting their ear to the railroad tracks. Those long, thin rails propagated the sound for miles. The low frequency (long wavelength) sounds went the furthest. Once I realized he was only describing transverse waves, I blurted out, "But there are two kinds of waves." He instantly understood and explained about his optics background, where he had only worked with one kind of wave. As a senior in college, I worked in a graduate student's optics lab, so I understood what he meant. My manager was pleased with me and said I probably had my first invention. He expected invention and had already shown me how to keep good lab book records.

Look at problems and solutions from a different angle. One of the lessons I learned from this experience is that different backgrounds are good. In fact, the case for diversity in business is not just a 'nice guy' thing, but rather it is a business imperative. Great breakthroughs come about when people of different backgrounds start talking and working together. As well as being my first invention, this was also my first opportunity as a new hire to mentor technically a seasoned employee. The kid straight out of college may know something you don't remember or never knew.

Work with other people. I usually have co-inventors. I need sounding boards. My best ideas happen as I talk them out with one or two others. It is exceedingly rare for me to submit an invention disclosure alone.

One way I keep from driving any one person nuts by demanding too much of their time, is to make sure I have multiple projects going with multiple people. Multiple projects allow your mind to play. You aren't constantly demanding that it think about only one thing.

Plan for future expansion instead of limiting your inventions. At my second standards meeting, I was asked whether the last free flag bit should be used to signal 'uncompressed mode selected'. My reaction was a strong, "No." Fortunately, I could articulate why. Later, I was asked my opinion on using the last free flag bit to signal 'another byte with more flags coming'. I strongly approved. Years later when I was involved with JPEG, I learned that more flag bits had been added until there were over 100. Old machines could tell when to stop when the final bit per byte signaled no more flags coming, but they ignored flags that signaled capabilities they didn't understand. The decoder told the encoder what its capabilities were and the encoder then chose a common set between machines. This is one of the first times I realized I had a talent for recognizing other people's great ideas.

Silliness Leads to Invention

Every book I have ever read about creativity emphasizes the need to suspend the critical analytic during brainstorming. It is important to have diversity on the team in order to avoid group-think. Even if the brainstorming only generates a well defined problem, don't be discouraged. Your mind continues to play with ideas, and in a few days or weeks, a solution pops out.

Silliness helps. A female colleague, educated in Beijing through college, was convinced she could not be creative. During a mentoring session, she agreed to try to be silly and within five minutes had correctly solved a problem I had been unsuccessfully working on for several months. When I asked her what had made the difference, she said she normally edited rather than voicing her ideas. She listened to a negative inner voice telling her she couldn't be right, so she discarded any ideas that came to her. When she gave herself permission to be silly, she found she could be creative. Since then she has been involved in multiple patent applications.

One common technique for suspending disbelief is to start with the question, "What if we put it on the moon?" Since this is generally considered politically, economically, and often technically impossible, the question sends people's thoughts into the realm of fantasy—where creative thinking takes place. My sister-in-law swears she raised her sons on science fiction and carefully explained to them that it is, in fact, possible to exceed the speed of light. We just haven't figured out how to do it yet.

My inventions often come to me as pictures. For example, I woke up one morning with a complete flow chart. I had been working on some code with five tests in the inner loop. It would have been impossible to debug. My new invention had only two tests. It took me a few hours to figure out how five decisions fit into a table with only two decisions. Sometimes I need my sounding board to 'read' what is in the boxes. The relative placement of the boxes and decision diamonds usually proves correct.

Let your unconscious mind do the work for you

When you need to invent, fill your head with lots of details and crazy ideas. Play with the concepts and do 'what if' mental experiments. It definitely helps to have someone to talk to who cares about the results. The early stages are mostly trying to define what a superior solution will look like. This is similar to asking the question, "If I knew what the answer was, what would it be?" Make sketches and notes. They may be useless, but they direct your creativity. Eventually you will know what properties the final answer must have in order to fill the need.

Once you reach this space, back off and don't do anything about it. Allow your idea to percolate. Read something, watch television, talk to a friend. Don't talk about the problem and don't try to think about the problem. Relax and go to sleep. When I do this, I frequently wake up during the night or the next morning with ideas flowing. Sometimes they come so fast I have to move quickly to capture them. After several hours of writing down ideas (mostly useful for the invention disclosure), I get dressed and go to work. On the way to work, as I think about the invention, major breakthroughs or simplifications occur.

Competition and collaboration can improve your invention

At one point, I hosted a company employee from the UK who wanted to use the mainframe to decode facsimile images. He was hoping for no worse than one second on the mainframe, although some image experts had told him to expect ten seconds. I assured him one second should be feasible. I had the advantage of knowledge because I had helped invent the data compression technique used to transmit the programmable character sets to the 3278 and 3279 host-attached display terminals.

The next time he came to the Research Center, more than a year later, he asked about 90 degree rotation using less than sixteen registers and one second for a facsimile page. We asked one of my experienced employees. I warned him the initial response would be something along the lines of, "What a stupid thing to do. Why would anyone want to do that?" At lunch, I posed the problem. It was hard not to laugh when my prediction was dead on, but the warning also took the offense out it. Fortunately, my employee was a good listener once we got past his initial statements. Knowing your employees, and their predictable reactions, makes management easier.

The next day I bumped into my employee. He asked when we were going to have the meeting. "I have the problem solved and I thought the UK employee might want to see it run in under a second." I rounded up the visitor and took him to the office where my employee demoed a simulation of rotating a facsimile image. E-mails went off to England, so a programmer there could code up the system.

At the next department meeting, my guy shared the problem and his solution. Then he offered to make his code available, and challenged anyone to improve on the execution speed. Several people took him up on it. They collaborated with him and within a week had a significant improvement, which also went off to the UK. They finished the presentation of their improvement at the next department meeting by issuing a similar challenge. This continued for several weeks, until the UK expert suggested we deliver object code to a simple interface. The final rotation code ran more than an order of magnitude faster than the original target.

Meanwhile, the UK guy started requesting other image processing algorithms. Except for me, the team first heard of the Image View Facility in the spring. By the following January, twelve patents had been filed before it was announced as an RPQ (Request Purchase Quotation). Most of the team received awards. I received my third Outstanding Innovation Award.

We were convinced we had the best 90 degree rotation algorithm possible. Some time later, an invention disclosure from our Kingston, New York plant crossed my desk for evaluation. When I understood enough to convince myself it would work, I called the inventor. I praised his brilliant invention and told him I was rating it file. Then he explained his management had already evaluated it "closed" as unimportant. My words were more than welcome as encouragement. His invention filed after some of my employees improved on it and joined him as co-inventors.

Allowing your mind to play

I do some of my best thinking when I let my mind wander undirected. For years, I kept a beach towel in my closet at work. Its purpose was to allow me to go outside and sit or lie under a tree. Our offices had no windows, so I couldn't stare outside and sometimes I had difficulty letting my mind wander. My beach towel was actually only used twice. There were many times when I gave myself permission to use it, but before I left my office I decided to get one pesky thing crossed off my 'to do' list so it would no longer clutter my mind. Before I knew it, quitting time had come and gone and I'd had an extremely productive day.

Creativity comes from allowing your mind to play. Inventing comes from identifying a problem and seeking a solution. Combine the two and you have successful inventions; novel solutions to problems. As I mentioned, I am more creative when working with others. Sometimes they supply the problem, sometimes they supply the answer, but I don't work well in a vacuum. And of course, I don't mind sharing the glory, either. Most of my inventions have been joint projects.

Find your own best style. Put a beach towel in your bottom drawer. Give yourself a focus point—a picture to stare at. Plug your tunes into your ears and find your zone. Talk to other people working on similar problems. Together you may be able to solve more than one. Never stop challenging your own assumptions and learning new ways to do things. If you find working with others distracts you and stops your creative process, perhaps you should work alone. Just be aware that by working alone you give up the opportunity to learn from someone else.

Summary

- Patents can be a money sink
- You can invent, so get started
- Silliness is part of creativity
- Sharing your ideas improves them

Part Three

Pulling it all Together

7

Change Your Mindset

Think Like an Owner

*I*n today's climate of outsourcing, it is important to think and act like an owner if you don't want to become a serf; trapped with no choices. Basic business finance cannot be ignored. JLM's Bookcase, a sole proprietorship mail order/tradeshow book business, taught me how to run a business, and at the same time, taught me I didn't want to be in charge of everything. I prefer working in a corporation big enough for my biggest ideas.

I saw trouble coming back in the late 80's, and started looking for a business that would give me great flexibility while still maintaining my interest. I quickly concluded most of retail demanded regular hours and therefore, was not to be considered. But the used and antiquarian book business would allow me to meet interesting people. Everyone I talked to agreed it would support you if you didn't have a mortgage. I intended to learn the trade while I could afford to make mistakes.

My secondary motivation was to understand how businesses operate. Too many people in big corporations have no sense of business. They can hide their mistakes and escape the consequences of poor decisions. Understanding business would help me appreciate the consequences of my errors.

The first thing I did was apprentice myself to a local antiquarian book dealer. I was willing to drive her van to trade shows and provide free labor in exchange for answers to questions. She soon realized I was serious and predicted I'd have a sole proprietorship before another year was out; long before I thought I would act.

The book business taught me many lessons—some of which I wish I had learned without making the mistakes. Lesson One: Inventory. I love buying books, always have. Most shopping I avoid, even grocery shopping, but I willingly drive two hours to a book store. Somehow, I had the idea I needed about 5,000 books before I could start selling. I accumulated those books in less than two years. Only then did I realize I had 5,000 different books and no desire to sell them.

They say some people are collectors and some are dealers. Collectors cannot part with their books while dealers know another great book is around the corner and are willing let one go when they find a buyer. It turns out I am neither. I had no trouble selling a book if I found a buyer; I just wasn't interested in looking for buyers.

I spent hours entering my books into the computer and printing labels, which I stuck on four by six cards and stored with the books. Lesson Two: Organization. I could instantly put my hands on the inventory control record for any book I owned.

As a business owner, the IRS looks unfavorably on your taxes if you have not made a profit after three years. It is hard to convince them you have a business and not a hobby. The IRS expects to find the signs of professionalism such as a business bank account, business insurance, and records. Lesson Three: Record Keeping. Those things I did well. I could easily prove how much I spent for any given volume, and when I did sell things, how much I sold them for. The IRS also expects you to sell.

Collapsible book cases are a wonder. They are light, easy to carry, and stack two high. I lined rooms with bookcases. Just about the time I had the books organized, there would be some reason the books all had to be moved—usually with helpers who didn't keep them in order. Re-stacking books became an ongoing activity.

When I moved to Vermont, the packers took the first day to pack my books—300 cases—and the second day to pack the house. While in Vermont, I experimented with having a few bookshelves in a place with other vendors. Lesson Four: Sales—the one I didn't master. Books sold, but I had trouble remembering to restock the shelves.

I kept putting off the sales part because I wanted to organize. Sales day never really arrived. When I went on unpaid leave of absence, I said, "Now I have no more excuses. I have time to put into the book business." But even when I had time, I didn't do it.

Many of my books eventually got stored in a basement. One winter day the electricity went out, the sump pump stopped and the sun warmed the snow. The resulting run-off ruined many cases of books. Lesson Five: Maintenance. I replaced the ones I missed (a few paperbacks) and wrote the others off.

Eventually I figured out what I should be doing, and the challenge vanished. The mechanics of being in the book business became just plain hard work. Not too long after that, I realized it was not the way I wanted to spend my life. I had enjoyed learning about the business for eight years. It may take another eight years to get rid of the books. Lesson Six: Passion—I didn't have it.

I moved to Colorado with only eighty cases of books. With a systematic effort to re-distribute the books (give them away), I moved into my house in Longmont five years later with about one thousand books. Fortunately, I have a one thousand square-foot unfinished basement. I bought additional collapsible bookshelves and lined two walls with books. At least the books are out of boxes. A friend recently sent me word that the library in New Orleans is looking for book donations. That should be good for a few cases.

What I 'should have' done

I short-circuited the apprenticeship program by becoming an owner and buying stock too soon. I did not make the acquaintance of other dealers and learn what sells. The purpose of running a book business is to sell books. I bought books. Most new dealers start out as 'scouts'. Scouts buy books on the weekends at tag sales, estate sales, and library sales. They have their favorite dealers. The high-class dealer will buy their best books, at a premium. The general dealer will take many books at a small increment over cost. The basement dealer will take everything—at a bargain. Graduate students can earn $100 a day without inventory, records, or storage issues. After they learn the business, they move to a mail order catalog business. If I had followed this model, I wouldn't have a thousand books in my basement, and I would have saved a ton of money.

One thing running a business did for me was to help me spot charlatans. A person who has run an actual business is great fun to talk with. They are interested in ways to improve business and cut paperwork. Fakers don't even understand paperwork is a problem. Fakers don't smile when you mention inventory. Fakers don't know how easily inventory eats up profits.

Running an unsuccessful business gave me insight into the problems businesses face today. Personally, I think Wall Street is much too enamored with downsizing as a solution to a company's problems. Companies are rarely stronger after downsizing, and there are now books out showing how and why downsizing doesn't work. However, as an owner I know salaries must be earned. I hired my sister. She did a better job than I did at organizing my inventory, but without income from selling the books, she became unaffordable.

I treat IBM as if it were my own business. This affects the way I spend its money (frugally) and spend my time. I know from personal experience that making money is hard work. I think on a different level when I think like an owner.

Dark times

I had a personal experience with downsizing that taught me a few things. About four PM on a Friday afternoon, I went to tell my Research manager good-bye and thank him. I thought I had arranged to come back after a week's vacation (selling books and attending the Data Compression Conference '94 in Snowbird, UT) to join another group. I left my manager's office in shock. Apparently, I had not transferred and I needed to find a new job. A few hours later, my manager stuck his head in my office and said, "You understood I meant you needed to find a new job in the company." I hadn't understood that at all.

I had been with the company nearly twenty years and the only retirement buy-out I remembered had taken place more than a decade before. That buy-out would have allowed me a multi-year 'leave of absence' bridge to retirement age. During the week in Snowbird, I considered my options, thinking I could bridge to retirement. My first impulse was to find another career where people wanted me. However, the rules had changed without me noticing. Retirement was not an option.

When I returned to Research, I learned this quickly. At Snowbird, I concluded the one thing I would find difficult to forgive would be losing my house to foreclosure. I put my house on the market and started downsizing as fast as I could.

I felt betrayed. Downsizing does that to you.

Four months later, a few days after I sold my house, the manager I thought I had transferred to (earlier in the year) asked if I was willing to talk to him and his boss. We met Friday afternoon. He said, "I understand you want an unpaid leave of absence." "Yep." I was being terse and non-committal. "Are you willing to leave immediately? Do you understand you will not have a job to return to? However, we will be glad to help you look for one when you return." "I am happy to leave immediately. I understand I have no job to return to. Your helping me look for one is more than I have now." By Monday morning, I'd been transferred. That is the fastest I've ever seen the paperwork processed. Without going into gory detail, I took that unpaid leave of absence, moved to Vermont to work on the MPEG book, and contracted to work part-time at our Burlington site.

I had other options. I could have gone into teaching. I could have moved to another company. For example, I interviewed for what appeared to be the perfect job for me. On the second day of interviews, I asked to meet with the company's systems expert. They didn't have one. I said, "I am the wrong person for your job. I don't have the one skill you need most." Later, I was invited to write my own job description and they would hire me for it. The offer helped ease my pain, but I decided to stick with what I knew.

Downsizing is not about individuals. I don't think it was a coincidence my house sold the same week I finally understood downsizing was not about me. Ten percent across-the-board-cuts don't look at individuals and their skills. Instead, the process spreads the pain over all departments with sweeping cuts. Once I started listening to conversations as if I were a third party, some of them were actually funny. As I thought like an owner, I understood how hard it was for the person on the other side of the desk. After all, I'd downsized my own sister because JLM's Bookcase could no longer afford her services, even though she was good at what she did.

I heard a definition of satisfaction and loyalty that I like and want to pass along. Satisfaction is, "How happy were you with the job we did?" Loyalty is, "How happy will you be to have us do your next job?" My suggestion to industry: Instead of 'laying off' highly valued employees, pay tuition and health insurance so they can afford to go back to school to retrain themselves. This spares them the shock and pain of being rejected, and leads to loyalty. When the time comes to refill those now vacant slots, you may wish to hire the experts you didn't need for a while. If you have engendered satisfaction and loyalty, they may be willing to come back.

Finances 101

A friend of mine once shared with me a saying from England from the time when ten pounds was a living wage for a family. "If you earn ten pounds a week and spend only nine, you're rich, but if you spend eleven, you're poor." This saying captures the concept of 'pay yourself first.' Some percentage of your paycheck, generally ten percent, should go directly into savings. Then figure out how to live on the rest. If you don't, the interest will soon mean you don't even have nine pounds left to live on. A good rule of thumb is to keep six month's salary in a liquid account. If disaster strikes, you will have enough to survive on while you get back on your feet.

If you don't save, at some point you will have to borrow. Heaven help you if you borrow on your credit card. Credit card interest can be as high as twenty-five percent. Someone recently described credit card debt as the failure to take out a bank loan. Bank loans can be negotiated. Generally, they are at least five percent less than credit card rates.

A friend asked for money management coaching. She was in serious credit card debt. The key to her turn-around was determining where she and her husband were living beyond their means. They both had good jobs. In this case, they were leasing an expensive car and truck every few years, so they were never out from under car payments. After talking it over, they decided to buy their vehicles at the end of the leases and in a few years, their car payments stopped.

The other key ingredient to resolving their financial issues was understanding compound interest. When you make a purchase and pay for it by borrowing (especially via your credit card), three things are happening:

1) You owe the credit card company interest until you pay off the debt,

2) You lose the interest you might have earned on the money if you had invested it instead of making the purchase, and

3) You decrease your ability to borrow in a crisis.

I encouraged them look at the final cost of purchases, not just the price tag. In some cases, they decided not to buy. Figure 1 is a graph illustrating monthly compound interest. In reality, interest is often compounded daily. Table 2 captures the same information in tabular form.

The rule of 72

If you want to know how many years it will take to double your money when it is earning compound interest, divide 72 by the interest rate and the answer is in years. Alternately, you can divide 72 by the number of years and determine the interest rate needed to double your money in the specified time. This is the 'rule of 72'. Before I understood the math, I had memorized, "At seven percent interest it will take ten years to double the money. At ten percent interest it will take seven years to double the money." Obviously, that was only one data point, but at the time the savings interest rate was around seven percent. The real power is not in the first doubling. The real power is being able to leave money invested long enough to obtain multiple doublings.

Figure 1. $10,000 Compounded Monthly

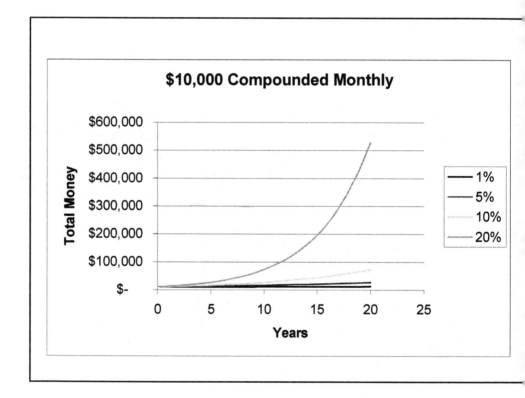

Table 2. $10,000 Compounded Monthly—Year End Totals

Years	1%	5%	10%	20%
0	$ 10,000	$ 10,000	$ 10,000	$ 10,000
1	$ 10,100	$ 10,512	$ 11,047	$ 12,194
2	$ 10,202	$ 11,049	$ 12,204	$ 14,869
3	$ 10,304	$ 11,615	$ 13,482	$ 18,131
4	$ 10,408	$ 12,209	$ 14,894	$ 22,109
5	$ 10,512	$ 12,834	$ 16,453	$ 26,960
6	$ 10,618	$ 13,490	$ 18,176	$ 32,874
7	$ 10,725	$ 14,180	$ 20,079	$ 40,087
8	$ 10,833	$ 14,906	$ 22,182	$ 48,881
9	$ 10,941	$ 15,668	$ 24,504	$ 59,606
10	$ 11,051	$ 16,470	$ 27,070	$ 72,683
11	$ 11,162	$ 17,313	$ 29,905	$ 88,628
12	$ 11,274	$ 18,198	$ 33,036	$ 108,073
13	$ 11,388	$ 19,130	$ 36,496	$ 131,783
14	$ 11,502	$ 20,108	$ 40,317	$ 160,695
15	$ 11,618	$ 21,137	$ 44,539	$ 195,950
16	$ 11,734	$ 22,218	$ 49,203	$ 238,940
17	$ 11,852	$ 23,355	$ 54,355	$ 291,361
18	$ 11,971	$ 24,550	$ 60,047	$ 355,283
19	$ 12,092	$ 25,806	$ 66,335	$ 433,229
20	$ 12,213	$ 27,126	$ 73,281	$ 528,275

Table 3 illustrates the value of starting early with your savings. Each time the value doubles, it starts from the total—including all previously compounded interest. What started out as $1,000 can increase to a healthy pot of change ($32,000) in five doublings.

Table 3. Multiple doublings of $1,000.00

Number of doublings	Value
0	$1,000
1	$2,000
2	$4,000
3	$8,000
4	$16,000
5	$32,000

Establish credit when you don't need it

Arranging for a bank loan is awkward when you are desperate. It is much easier to establish a relationship with the bank before you need it. When I moved to Boulder, I asked for twice the normal overdraft protection. The bank made me come back and ask again a year later. I did so because my credit card was on auto payment and its credit limit was twice the normal protection. This time the bank granted my request. Having the extra credit—and not abusing it—helped me when I wanted a home mortgage in less time than it normally takes to get a credit card.

In college and graduate school, I didn't own a car so I tore up the offers for gas cards. Once I got a regular job, I bought a car and applied for a gas card. I wanted a particular card because the station was on my way to work and had good prices. The first time I was rejected, I assumed I'd failed to fill out the application properly. The second time I wondered where I might have made a mistake. By the third time, I was sure I'd done nothing wrong and the problem had to be with the gas company.

I had read a magazine column about asking for more information when you are turned down on a credit application. According to the article, a supervisor has more authority to tell you the facts, so I insisted on talking to the supervisor. I requested information on my, obviously false, bad credit. She replied, "You don't have bad credit, you have no credit— that can sometimes be worse." Then she explained, "You must have at least three credit cards. I can see you have one VISA card. All you need to do is go to two local stores, take out a credit card, buy something, and pay it back early or on time. In six months, apply again." Having a good job simply didn't count and until the store cards were actually used, they were useless in establishing credit. If you have no credit, apply for a couple of store cards. Most department stores will issue the cards on the spot.

Too many women have joint credit with their spouses, but nothing in their own name. If all of your credit is through your husband, what happens if he is no longer in the picture? You could find yourself with no credit. And even worse, if your spouse is not responsible, you could find yourself saddled with his bad credit rating. The nightmare of trying to rehabilitate your credit is an experience you don't want, and going through it when the bad credit isn't even yours makes the situation much worse.

Face your financial difficulties

Like everyone else, I've made investment mistakes. One summer I had two mortgages to pay. I knew I had an award coming to get me out of my cash crunch, and thought I could wait it out. I calculated my expenses, including lunch money. Lunch was my main meal, and I bought it in the cafeteria. My weekly grocery bill, even once in a month, would have been enough to bounce my mortgage check, so I ate what was in the house. I didn't tell anyone about my situation, although I thought a church friend suspected. She and I met to practice reading on Saturday morning, and almost every week there was a reason I should go home with her for lunch and then stay for dinner to enjoy family games in the evening. The same thing happened on Sundays. She usually insisted I take leftovers home. Twenty years later, I told her my situation and asked if she had guessed. She remembered the summer, because I was tutoring her children, but had no idea about my financial situation. Her natural generosity fed me all summer.

About September of that year, I realized I had to quit looking to that award check for financial salvation. I took steps to rent one of my spare rooms. Soon a company employee asked to rent for two weeks. Since her rent check covered the groceries, I started buying them again.

Who knows how long I would have continued to depend upon the kindness of friends if she hadn't come along? I only know I was grateful to have friends who would feed me when I needed to be fed. I let pride keep me from admitting my situation, but the food came to me anyway.

With the crisis over, someone suggested I should ask the bank to accept a 'deed in lieu'. My real estate partners and I could offer to give the bank ownership of the property in lieu of making the mortgage payments. This would save them a year of legal hassles and get us out from under the mortgage.

The bank officer I talked to was gracious. When I thanked her, she explained the bank is pleased to work with people who tell them what the problem is rather than just walking away and not letting them know there is a problem. She asked each of us to write a letter explaining the special circumstances. She told me I could stop paying the mortgage immediately, but to keep up the association fees. I could manage the condo fees.

Eventually the bank asked us to put the condo on the market and try to sell it for six months. If at the end of six months it hadn't sold, they would accept the deed in lieu. The condo had been on the market, but our real estate agent had disappeared. I asked the bank for the name of the agent they dealt with. We listed the condo for sale and were happy to sign it over to the bank six months later.

When you find yourself facing serious financial difficulties, don't hide from them. Ignoring serious problems rarely causes them to go away. Seek advice from family and friends. Consult with your banker or other financial advisor. Keep in touch with your lenders. Most lenders are willing to work with you to resolve a situation, but only if you take the first step and let them know what's going on.

Inflation

Many people count on inflation to wipe out their debts (effectively) by allowing them to pay back with cheaper money. Do you really wish inflation on your children and grandchildren? Cheaper money means your savings lose value. I'd rather not encourage inflationary forces.

I have a second cousin (once or twice removed) in England who found herself fighting those inflationary forces. On one visit, she explained she had to spend her paycheck the instant she received it, before the things she might someday want became more expensive. There was no counter space left in her kitchen because gadgets took all the space, and except for her first few purchases, she didn't need, use, or even enjoy most of the things she felt obliged to purchase before her paycheck lost its value.

Using leverage

I read in the paper about 'leveraging' to manage your money. Leveraging means you use a little of your own money and borrow the rest. When you sell, you get a great return on investment because after you return the bank's money, profit is calculated relative to your money.

Of course, the counter example of losing lots of money (all of yours and more of the bank's) is rarely mentioned. The bank expects you to pay them back even if you didn't make money. This is called 'risk'. I have discovered I have a relatively low risk-tolerance for areas where I don't have a passionate interest. The older I get, and the closer I get to retirement, the less interest I have in taking significant risks.

Most financial experts will tell you leverage is a sound financial principal. If you are young and just starting to invest and earn, you may be able to obtain outstanding returns using leverage. If you lose instead of earning money, you still have years to recover from your mistakes. On the other hand, if you are nearing retirement, your earning years are limited. Leverage becomes much riskier. Consult with your financial advisor and weigh the risks carefully.

Of course, a home mortgage is just one example of using leverage. Some of your money, and more of the bank's money. When the value of the house appreciates and you sell, the profit is all yours.

When I bought my home in Colorado, I decided I wanted to be mortgage free by my earliest likely retirement date—about five years out. Monday morning, I walked into my bank and asked to talk to someone about an unconventional fixed rate mortgage where I put 40% down, amortized for five years, and took out an equity line of credit at the same time. Oh, and it would be convenient to close on Friday.

Thanks to information from my real estate agent, I had with me statements from all bank accounts, my last two years of income tax returns, a copy of my salary statement, a handwritten explanation of the source of funds for the down payment, and the draft sales contract.

A bank officer showed me into a conference room and started out telling me my idea was impossible, but asked to see my documentation and suggested I fill out the application. I knew there was hope when he asked permission to organize my paperwork. About halfway through, he left to make copies of everything. He also made inquiries about my credit rating and history with his bank. He came back to tell me an appraisal had been arranged for the next day, and we could close on Friday. The whole process took 40 minutes. He recommended a conventional Variable Rate mortgage with no points. The first five years, the loan had a fixed interest rate. If I had difficulties paying off the loan, the variable rate would kick in and my shortfall wouldn't embarrass me.

The reason I went to my bank first is that I'd walked in two weeks before and been well treated. I needed to know when a large check from a land sale would clear so I could write checks against it. The bank manager became involved in the decision. After confirming I had owned the land outright, seeing my paperwork from the title company, and finding the security writing that assured them this was an original check, his answer was, "Now." He engendered my loyalty, and earned my future business.

It's all a matter of choices

My first salary was four times as much as my graduate school assistantships, but prices were eight times higher. Moving from a college campus to Westchester County in New York State gave me sticker shock. I paid a quarter for the movies on campus. Three dollars for a movie ticket seemed outlandish. I felt poor.

Finally, one day I realized I had a 'poor' attitude and it needed to change. I replaced, "Can I afford to do this?" with, "Do I really want to do this, because if I do, I can afford it." The answer was frequently, "No, I have absolutely no desire to do it." I used money as an excuse to avoid doing things. That's when I sat down and figured out what I wanted to do. I went into New York City and saw three plays in a weekend. Giving myself permission to do what I wanted to do made a huge difference in my life. I felt rich instead of poor.

In Boulder, I enjoy eating with a group who pack their lunches every day. They have made a conscious choice to spend several dollars less per day. If they save $4 per day, they have chosen not to spend around $1000 per year on lunches. I make the choice to buy my lunch. In our cafeteria, the servings are large enough I can save half the lunch and have it for dinner later in the week. Even the small choices you make can have a major impact on your financial situation. Look at what you have decided—consciously or unconsciously—to do and examine your choices. Are they the best ones for you?

My landlady once asked for help in figuring out why she couldn't stay within her budget. She knew her household expenses and the total was less than her take home pay, yet she always had to borrow money to pay her local school taxes. We sat down together, and several hours later determined her spending was out of control in three places: buying three coffees a day at work, paying for restaurant dinners for two more often than she could afford, and using credit cards to borrow the difference.

Between us, we found simple solutions to her situation. Since it had not occurred to her to save enough each month to cover non-monthly expenses, such as the school taxes, the extra money in her checking account led to unwise purchases. She arranged with her bank to transfer 1/52nd of her annual tax bill, her yearly insurance, her estimated car maintenance, and enough money for Christmas and vacations, into her savings account every week. By taking a thermos of her favorite coffee to work, she saved most of the nine dollars a day (about $2,000 per year) she spent at the coffee cart. She didn't even like coffee-cart coffee, but bought it to be social. Finally, if she stopped buying alcohol with her meals out, she could still afford to dine out once a week.

Keeping in mind the story of the English workman who made ten pounds per week but spent eleven, she was pleased to find her lifestyle only needed a small correction. She dedicated my rent check to paying off her credit cards and growing her savings. Not buying coffee at work and being more frugal on the meals out helped to pay for daily living expenses. Several years later, she told me that after our discussion she was able to quit worrying about her finances. Her take-home pay only had to last for monthly living expenses. The non-monthly expenses came out of savings, and she had enough money saved to cover them. She was even able to put money into CDs so she got a better interest rate. She timed them to come due at tax time, or insurance renewal time or Christmas or vacation time. If you find yourself running out of money before you run out of month, take a look at your 'extra' expenses. Do you go out for coffee more often than you can afford? Do you regularly order a bottle of wine with your dinner out?

Budgets

Living within your means requires making a budget and sticking to it. You don't actually have to write your budget out, but it helps. I've never had much luck making a budget because I fail to include non-monthly expenses like car insurance, time share maintenance fees, car maintenance, charitable donations, and discretionary travel. You know what your expenses are each month, and you know what additional expenses you have. When you estimate your monthly budget, remember to include a pro-rata share of these non-monthly expenses as well. Have as many payments as possible on auto-debit. Only put money in your checking account that you can spend. Everything else goes directly into savings. That way, you have the funds to cover insurance and so on when they come due, and anything left over in your checking account at the end of the month really is available for extras. Don't buy extras until the end of the month.

Indulgences

The summer I didn't buy groceries, I visited a family whom I was helping to purchase a home. They were having trouble making the house payments, but I watched the children snack on avocados (at least $1 each) and leave half-finished juice bottles lying around. Their mom explained she was from Puerto Rico and she wanted her children to have the fruits she grew up with. I realized our deal was likely to go sour. They wasted more groceries during the time I visited than I bought that summer. People who want everything now are unlikely to have anything later. And of course, if I had been thinking like an owner, I would have taken steps to correct the situation— although what steps I might have taken, I can't say. As an owner, they were wasting my resources.

Everyone has at least one indulgence. Figure out what yours is, and plan for it in your budget. That way, you won't be surprised by a shortfall. When I started earning my own money, I made a decision to indulge in books. It didn't take me long to figure out hardbound books take a lot of storage space, and storage space was scarce in dorm rooms. I generally wait for the paperback editions, but I buy all the books I want. When someone says to me, "You don't drink, smoke, or do drugs, you must have no indulgences," I remind myself, "Yes I do. My indulgence is books." It's an expensive hobby, but I gave myself permission years ago to indulge in it.

Credit reports

You should look at your credit report at least once a year. It may be the only warning you get if someone steals your identity and runs up your bills. I've seen newspaper advertisements advising readers they can order a free credit report once a year. This is one of those 'do as I say, not as I do' lessons.

The last time I asked for a credit report was a horrible experience. When I refinanced my mortgage, the bank requested I get a credit report. That was their way of informing me I had credit problems. When the report arrived, two unpaid credit card totals from stores in the Midwest were spoiling my credit. The local address was not mine and the name was "Joann Mitchell" instead of "Joan Mitchell." I called the stores to ask if they could help me clear up my report. One store was helpful. I gave them my social security number and they confirmed it did not match the credit card application of the offending card. The other store was decidedly unhelpful. I offered to pay the unpaid amount. They would not allow me to pay the bill, although they were willing to leave it on my credit report.

The point is, you don't know what's on your credit report unless you look at it. If you check it annually, you have the opportunity to clear up erroneous information before it stops you from doing what you want to do. It can also open your eyes to the amount of outstanding credit/debt you have, and give you time to head in a better direction financially.

Credit card applications arrive almost daily. Too much credit can be as fatal as no credit or bad credit. In calculating your credit total, the maximum limits of all your credit cards are summed. Limit yourself to three major cards and one or two store cards, otherwise your FICO score may drop and you will pay higher interest rates.

Every time you pay a bill late—even a few days late—it shows up on your credit report. I vividly remember a relative asking my dad for advice. She always paid her bills in pairs to save a postage stamp every other month. This practice resulted in a poor credit rating, so when she attempted to obtain home mortgage financing, she faced difficulties. Fortunately, when she stopped trying to save a few cents on postage, began making monthly payments monthly, and wrote a letter of explanation, she was able to qualify for her mortgage.

Minding your business

I asked a financial planner for advice on becoming more knowledgeable about the stock market. She recommended I subscribe to *Barron's*, a weekly financial newspaper. I followed her advice for several years, but never succeeded in forcing myself to read beyond the first page. Definitely not my idea of fascinating reading material. On the other hand, if you read it, you can learn to manage your investments.

If you don't want to read *Barron's* and become a financial expert, you should seek out the advice of a professional. Since your financial advisor will manage your money, you should find someone you work well with. They should listen to you. They should have values similar to yours. You should trust them.

Be very careful about 'hot tips.' Early in my investment career, my broker broke her own rule and passed along a hot tip. It paid off well, in both appreciation and earnings. The next year, I invested more in the same stock. This time the company went bankrupt. My broker and I concluded there was a high probability the stock had been manipulated by distributing exceptional earnings in order to raise the price one year, and then disappearing with the stockholders' money the next year.

I once tried to interest a relative in a 'sure deal'. His answer was, "If it is so sure, why do they need investors? The company can finance itself by growing a little bit slower. Let the promoter keep the wealth in his family." He was right, and this was my most expensive education.

Finding an investment counselor you can work with isn't always easy. My first financial planner actually advised me to "save less money" only a few months before I was downsized. Fortunately, I didn't listen to him. He left the business, and his replacement wouldn't listen to me. After I sold my home in New York, the money from the sale sat in the bank while I looked for another advisor.

During my trips from Illinois to Burlington, I stayed at a hotel. At one of their happy hour events, I met a school teacher whose mother had gone back to school when the kids were through college. Mom finished her degree, and became a stock broker for a large, well-known firm. My new friend commented, "My mom is passionate about helping other people make money. I'll be a millionaire when I retire thanks to Mom investing my savings for me." I made an appointment to meet her mother the next time she and I were in town at the same time.

Mom and I clicked. Her opening was along the lines of, "I want to make clear up front that I don't deal in junk or penny stocks. I'm conservative. If speculating in the market is your main goal, I'm not the broker for you." I liked the fact she always told me what she thought, including, "You're nuts not to invest in industry xxx, but it's your money so tell me what you want to do." She listened. She gave me advice, but accepted my decisions without arguing. Of course, this led to a great working relationship.

Buying a car

Buying a car can be an easy process if you know what you want. When I bought my second new car, I checked out several dealerships and found problems with the cars, such as not being able to see over the hood. Selecting the right car can be a time-consuming process, but it's a necessary step in getting what you need.

After you decide what brand fits you, you need to select a sales person. Hang around the sales area and watch the way the sales people work until you find one who seems likeable. Once again, this process may take some time, but it will make the experience less stressful for you.

Value your time wisely and think like an owner. Purchase what is necessary to make your company (your life) operate smoothly.

Summary

- Treat company resources carefully
- Think like an owner
- Beware of compound interest on debt
- Embrace compound interest on savings
- Establish credit in your own name
- Know where your money goes
- Establish a relationship with your banker before you need it

8

Outside the Job

*W*hat happens at home has a big impact on productivity at work. Your support system away from work should include people who care about you and don't expect you to entertain them. Some people find those friends at church or in a social club, others seek out neighbors. Giving back to the community is essential to creating a living environment that regenerates rather than depletes.

I first asked the question, "Is success worth it?" after hearing what an executive told my future brother-in-law's class at Wharton Business School. He claimed the entire Research Division where I worked was supported so one out of ten researchers would do something significant in one out of ten years. I remember thinking, "Even if I am that one out of ten, what about those nine out of ten years?" That was when I decided to quit trying to succeed 100% of time. Instead, I did work-related volunteer work. That way I could go home every night knowing I had made a difference for someone even when my research was a long, slow process and the results might not yet be apparent.

Work/life balance

Challenging experiences balancing work and personal life don't suddenly become important on your first job. My junior year at the university I graded 120 papers three times a week. Although Dad paid for most of our undergraduate education, he required us to have a job so we would appreciate the value of a dollar. I was taking challenging courses like Quantum Mechanics and Electricity & Magnetism as I started the year-long sequence of Differential Equations. I had a problem set due every day. Since I couldn't do the math, I had to turn in the problem sets half-finished. I turned them in an hour after class no matter the status. After all, another set was due the next day.

Whenever someone proposed an extracurricular activity, I asked myself, "Is this an activity I really want to do?" If the answer was "Yes," I'd participate regardless of the state of my homework. If I didn't really want to play, I'd say "No" and refuse to be talked into it. I enjoyed going out for pizza or for a movie part of the time, but not every night. But, I made sure I didn't put happiness on hold until the pressure was off.

I went home the night before Thanksgiving of my junior year and couldn't sleep. I got up to tell my parents I was going to flunk all my classes. I knew I wouldn't be kicked out of school. Their reaction was, "Was it worth it?" I answered, "Yes." I had insisted on going to England for the winter and spring quarters of my sophomore year, and then traveled through Europe the following summer. As a result of my time overseas, I took all my full-year sequences concurrently during my junior year. My physics advisor had me skip most of the sophomore classes and arranged for me to enter the advanced physics program. That meant I was taking classes out of order and hadn't had the math for Quantum Mechanics.

One by one, I studied for finals and mastered the material. Then, I got to the Quantum Mechanics course. It was my last final. I visited the professor to confirm I'd finally 'gotten it'. I shocked him because I had everything wrong. After I explained the coursework used math still two quarters away in my schedule, he calmed down. I promised to drop the class and pick it up a year later. On my final, I correctly set up the equations for all eight questions, but had to the leave the rest blank because I didn't know how to work the math. If I hadn't visited the professor, I'd have flunked his course.

The time spent overseas was worth the risk. I kept my work in balance with my life.

As an aside, I attended the 35th reunion of my Stanford in England (Britain III) group. We lived at Harlaxton Manor near Grantham in Lincolnshire. Some of us tried to figure out why 95% of our Britain III group responded in some way and almost half made it. It seemed to hinge on inclusiveness. I felt free to join any group at meals. We also put on two plays in which almost everyone contributed. At the previous reunion, I had mentioned my involvement with the JPEG committee to several people. They were mystified. At the 35th reunion, it was fun for me to hear they were now using JPEG frequently.

When I moved to Boulder, I gave myself permission to work less and spend more time keeping work and life in balance. One way I arranged to work less was to take up scuba diving. I consciously looked for an activity that didn't require pre-planning and that I would enjoy with other people. Since I love being in the water, scuba was a possible match.

I bought snorkel equipment and signed up for scuba lessons. Early in February, after open water dives in Homestead Springs, Utah, I received my certificate. In March, I bought the rest of my gear, and did my Advanced Open Water Certification during a week of diving in Cozumel, Mexico. My adventures during my first ocean scuba diving were published in my high school alumni newsletter.

Building Your Support Network

Your support system away from work includes people who care about you and don't expect you to entertain them. I first heard the term 'refrigerator friends' at a humorous lecture on "Road Rage." The speaker shared his experience at a family reunion where a distant cousin helped himself to drinks from the refrigerator without having to ask permission. After that, he offered his friends 'refrigerator privileges'. Friendships are more relaxed when no one has to entertain.

For me, holidays are times for big meals and lots of family. In my family, women tend to congregate in the kitchen and the guys in front of the television watching a game, so my idea of a great get-together is being able to participate in the kitchen work. Recently a friend invited me to Thanksgiving with his family and friends. Things were a little topsy turvy because they had been redecorating—including painting. Many things were still packed away in the basement. I felt right at home when his wife didn't insist very hard that I stay out of her kitchen. I enjoyed making the vegetable tray, and later, doing the dishes. It was a great day. I was invited back a few weeks later for Christmas. This time they assumed I would help out in the kitchen and I had another great day.

Some people find close friends at church or in a social club. Since graduate school, I make a point of joining the local church as soon as possible. In Colorado, I've joined a group who go out to lunch every Sunday after the service. Frequently, several of us buy season tickets for the local Theater. Over lunch, it's easy to invite each other to local events. These friendships insure there is always someone to whom I can turn, whether I need something material—you may recall I ate for the summer with one of my church friends when I didn't have grocery money—or only companionship.

A strong support network can help you handle frustration. I have friends at work whom I trust not to overreact when I walk into their offices and say, "May I vent? Please don't take me too seriously, but I need to dump my frustrations." Once I air my complaints, I often recognize the real problem and am back in solution mode. Of course, those friends know they can count on me for the same thing. When they need to vent, or when they need advice, they feel free to drop in.

I used to think the more experience I had, the smoother my work and life would become. Life doesn't work that way. One of my early mentors taught freshman calculus, and I graded papers for her as a junior. We keep in touch. She told me how bumpy her experience became after the department chair, who also valued teaching, left. They taught most of the founders in Silicon Valley, so she has received offers at much bigger salaries, but she loves teaching. As she described her experiences, all I could think was, "What if she had left before I arrived?" Her experience has helped me through many rough spots.

Giving Back to the Community

Everyone chooses their own path in giving back to the community. Some people work with children, some with the economically disadvantaged, and some with the physically or mentally challenged. When you make 'giving back' a part of your life, you gain much more than you give.

Giving back to the community is essential to maintaining true communities. For several years, I worked at becoming a scuba-buddy for the handicapped. One year I tutored a sixth-grader in reading. More recently, I helped organize a pot luck picnic for my Home Owner's Association. When my town had a day devoted to considering its future, I was pleased to participate. It really doesn't matter what you do as long as you participate and work to make life better for the members of your community.

A hobby of mine (begun while I was in graduate school and renewed in Colorado) is teaching people afraid of water how to float. The students I met in Accessible Waves (a nonprofit established to help the physically handicapped learn to scuba dive) weren't afraid of water, so it generally took only one or two sessions before they were able to pass the ten-minute float test for scuba. One example of success was a man who said he had not floated or swum without flotation devices since becoming wheelchair bound. During our first session, he discovered he could float on his back, on his front, and roll over from back to front to back unassisted. The next week he learned, or remembered, how to swim. He had no trouble passing the float test and the 200-yard swim.

Learning to swim

When I was seven, and for the next three summers, Mom dropped me, some neighborhood kids, and some of my sisters off at a public pool once a week for swimming lessons. I started the class able to go off the low dive head first, was a reasonable dog-paddler, and was fearless in the water. You had to swim (with your face in the water) half-way across the width of the pool in order to move to the next class. I remember getting within two feet of the goal on my first try and never coming close again. Talk about humiliation! All my friends passed out of the beginning class in one session and left me behind.

When I was ten, Mom arranged for a neighborhood teenager with a backyard pool to give me private lessons before summer started. I finally got the idea of taking a breath by rotating my head to the side instead of sinking as my mouth reached up for air. Once I understood the idea, I could learn to swim.

That year, immediately after school, we went to Laguna Beach, where I had a near-drowning experience. I ran out to catch a wave so it would carry me back in, but had to duck under it. After the third wave (all of which I had to go under, to my great disappointment), the water was over my head when I came up. I stayed calm and was grateful I could swim. After trying to swim in and realizing I was drifting further out to sea, I asked a nearby bodysurfer for help. He tried unsuccessfully and called upon two of his friends to assist as well. The three of them couldn't move me toward shore. Finally, the lifeguard decided to help. The lifeguard was there in just a few strokes, clamped me under his arm, and we shot through the water. He gave me a scolding and made me promise not to go swimming alone again. I didn't even try to explain. I was just grateful to be out of the water.

Shortly thereafter, my parents joined a new Swim and Racquet Club. The instructors (and owners) were swim coaches and under their group instruction, I rapidly moved through beginning and intermediate classes to finish the summer as an advanced swimmer.

Teaching people afraid of the water to float

Early in my graduate-school years, I was sitting on the floor at a party when I overheard two friends making arrangements to buy swimming suits together. Curious, I asked why they both needed swim suits. They each told me about near-drowning experiences much more serious than mine, and went on to say they were determined to get over it and learn to swim. I offered to help, explaining how I still remembered the humiliation of not being able to learn to swim, and going on to explain how I became an advanced swimmer in one summer.

My friends bought swim suits and we met at the campus pool a few days later. We developed a poolside exercise. I had both women place their fingers on the side of the pool. Then they placed their feet flat on the side of the pool with their legs bent so their knees were on their chests. Their bodies only lifted about a half inch on the first try.

I noticed both were 'non-dentable'. By this I mean, a poke with a finger didn't dent the flabby parts by at least a half inch. It was like poking iron. So I asked them to lie on their backs on the cement apron. Then I told them to pretend they were floating on clouds. I kept up a running patter until I saw their arms and legs relax. The poke test worked.

We returned to the pool, and when the water raised them three inches during deep breathing exercises, I knew they were ready to float. This was the first time my friends had felt the water lift them. They had tried to force themselves to stay on top instead of trusting the water to hold them up.

I demonstrated how body position matters in floating. I started out floating on my back on the surface of the water. Then I took a good breath, dropped my hips, and sank to the bottom. When I elevated my hips, I returned to the surface. Many new swimmers think they have to hold their body rigid and flat on the surface in order to float. This translates into their feet being out of water and their bodies tense. Instead, I suggested their legs should act like "Jell-O" or a "Raggedy Ann" doll—limp and loose with no tension.

My friends quickly expanded the network, bringing other non-swimmers or non-floaters to join our sessions. By the end of graduate school, I had taught thirteen students how to float.

Further opportunities

I was in Toronto in November 2001, attending a weekend workshop I had helped to organize on the Digital Divide. I joined a group of employees for dinner and learned one of the ladies (tall and thin) was unable to float. She was going to the Caribbean with her family and really didn't want to watch from the beach again. Her husband was into scuba and snorkeling.

Another woman offered to lend her a bathing suit, and the next morning we met at 6 AM at the hotel pool. By the end of our first session, my new friend was thrilled. She had felt the water hold her up. We had another session the next morning. She mastered floating and we moved on to basic swimming.

The workshop organizer saw my new friend return the swim suit and overheard her glorious descriptions of newfound freedom to enjoy the water. Three years later, at another company event, he introduced me to a friend of his and suggested we go swimming together. It took me a while to figure out she needed a floating lesson. I thoroughly enjoyed the experience. The great thing about teaching adults is they listen and can articulate how they feel about your instructions.

Dive certifications

At one point, I agreed to be a scuba-buddy on an ocean trip for a person in a wheelchair. I realized I had no idea what to do if I couldn't put my feet on the bottom of the pool. This convinced me to complete the PADI Rescue Diver course. I didn't care if I passed the course, but I wanted the knowledge and training. My instructor believes it's okay to direct others to help you, so instead of having to get a 200-pound person onto a dock two feet above water alone and while wearing full scuba gear, I was able to supervise two willing helpers, and together we did it easily.

My unexpected success with the Rescue Diver course encouraged me to enroll in the PADI Dive Master course. As a Dive Master Candidate, I had to observe and help out with ten pool sessions. Every class had someone who needed help floating. My instructor bragged about me ahead of time because he was confident someone would be an instant sinker. Since I had a 100% success rate, he no longer believed body type made it impossible for some people to float.

The year I decided to pass my Dive Master requirement to swim sixteen timed laps, I joined the Longmont Masters swimmers. They met at 6:30 AM several times a week. The coach heard me talking about teaching people who are afraid of water how to float. At her invitation, I started helping her with disabled children once a week.

Find your own path

I enjoy the water, and I developed my techniques for teaching people to float over several decades. You probably have a talent for something as well. Just keep in mind, what seems trivial to you may be terribly important to someone else. If you do something you enjoy doing, you will find opportunities to share your expertise. Take advantage of the opportunities. You may be able to change someone's life. At the very least, you will be able to make a new friend and further develop your talent.

Giving back to the community does not require you to do 'big' things. Giving back requires you to do 'little' things. You may be able to devote one morning or afternoon a week to delivering 'Meals on Wheels' or to reading stories to children at the local library. You can pound nails with 'Habitat for Humanity' or man a crises intervention hot line. The things you do, no matter how large or small, affect people's lives. Give generously.

Giving Back at Work

About eighteen months into my job, I was going home each night unhappy and dissatisfied. I need to interact with people, but had become isolated in the lab and was not talking to anyone outside my small group. I made a conscious decision to quit trying to be a success and to give ten percent of my working time (tithe) to volunteer work.

I chanced upon the department secretary—we didn't call them assistants back then—in the hall and asked her if anyone needed tutoring. After a moment's hesitation, she asked if I could teach people how to use the computer. "Yes," I eagerly responded, and then asked if she knew someone who needed help. "Me," was her answer.

Several months before, just before Christmas, many of the secretaries had been given a week of half-day computer training. They were not backfilled, so they left the class and went back to their stations to a full day's work. The computer terminals were finally arriving, and the secretaries were petrified they wouldn't be able to use them. They had been told they would get a black mark in their personnel jackets at the end of the year if they weren't computer literate on the word processor and able to perform tasks assigned.

Our first session was aimed at getting her over her fear of the computer and her fear she couldn't learn it. We agreed to meet during lunch hour and work together at her desk but that didn't work well, so our next two sessions were after work. I uncovered three problems:

1) she was terrified she could hurt the computer,
2) she was unaware of the different layers within the computer and the different commands each layer required, and
3) she was unaware there was a difference between 'input' and 'edit' modes inside the word processor.

Once she was over her fear, we worked on understanding the 'layers of the onion'. I drew a big onion on her board and labeled the layers "CP" (Central Processor), "CMS" (Command Monitor System), "Editor," "Edit Mode" and "Input Mode." Then I showed her where to look to determine which layer she was in. I drilled her by having her close her eyes, I'd get the computer to some state, and she had to figure out where she was. Then I'd ask her to move to another state. Sometimes it required a two layer move. I felt her eagerness building as she learned how to get in (and out) of the computer.

Our last session was a refresher course, moving through her week's lessons. She had mastered the layers, knew which commands happened during edit mode (such as 'file' and 'save'), and realized she had to be in input mode to type things into a file. She knew the course material. Within a week she was showing me output more sophisticated than anything I ever attempted.

I was a bit disappointed her need was met in just three hour-long sessions, so I was pleased when she sent me off to the private secretary of a Nobel Prize winner. He happened to be out of town so we could work any time. It only took two sessions. Next, I helped out the semi-private secretary to two Fellows. She was done in one session. I asked her what her bosses did. "Whatever they want."

That was how I learned about the Fellow position. I went home and wrote out my goal to become the first female IBM Fellow. I eventually became the seventh female Fellow.

I've made many of my more important contacts while doing give-back. Once I decided to make give-back a part of my life, I learned the local Sigma Xi chapter was looking for someone to volunteer for the office of Secretary. IBM allowed the local chapter free use of the auditorium and allowed them to invite the public to evening talks aimed at educating people in the field of science. The cafeteria served dinner an hour before these meetings, and many people invited their families to come to dinner and the talk.

The officers met regularly and supported each other. As Secretary, I took the minutes of these meetings and distributed the posters, to advertise our sponsored talks. The treasurer was a perennial volunteer who managed the money. We could ask outside speakers and offer them an honorarium about half the time. When I became Vice Chair for a year, I filled in as needed. As Chair, I was empowered to invite the speakers. These were usually world-class scientists from both inside and outside the company. At one level, the job was scary. At another level, it was exhilarating to be hosting these scientists for an evening.

People's perceptions of me changed when they saw me on the stage comfortably introducing the speaker. During dinner, I tried to learn some fact that would be interesting to the crowd. The dinner table discussion got everything off to a good start, and then I could 'wow' the crowd with my newly acquired information. One evening, during the final days before an international standards meeting, I was on the stage to introduce our speaker. I kept saying 'biological' when the word I wanted was 'biographical'. After a few unsuccessful tries, I looked at the audience, confessed I'd been up for 72 hours straight, and said, "I'm sure you know the word I mean." The audience cracked up and the lecture proceeded smoothly.

My thesis advisor was one of our guest speakers, so I picked him up at the airport. He had written a book called *How Everyday Things Work*. Our conversation on the way to the site profoundly changed my attitude towards management. He convinced me management is not a prestige job, but a service position. After this conversation, and considerable reflection and further discussion with others in my support network, I decided I was ready to take on the challenge.

At the Center for Advanced Studies Conference (CASCON) in Toronto, Canada, I gave the keynote address one year. My talk was, "The Importance of Giving Back and Reaching Back." I had been appointed a company Fellow that year, and was looking back over my career and seeing a strong correlation between people I met while doing 'give back at work' and people who helped to promote me later.

As a Research Staff Member (RSM) on assignment in Boulder, the site Technical Vitality Council (TVC) invited me to their monthly brown-bag lunch meetings. After I had attended a few times, they asked me to be the liaison with the Academy of Technology since I was one of two members on site, and the current liaison was ready to pass the baton. Since there is a full-time facilitator, I enjoy inviting out-of-town company employees who are visiting the area to speak. I particularly look for Academy members to introduce to the Boulder engineers. After the proposed speakers submit their talk abstract and bio, the facilitator can be counted upon to handle the rest of the logistics well.

At one of the monthly TVC luncheons, we went around the room introducing ourselves. To my shock, I was seated next to a PhD from my division whom I had never met. She had finished her PhD four months earlier. We clicked immediately. Within a few months, we had filed five patent applications with a third inventor. I made a point of introducing her to the top technical female in the company and they had lunch together. Having someone help her get ahead was a new experience for her. A year later, she became a Research Staff Member and transferred to the Research Division.

The TVC puts on the technical awards dinner each year. During one of these dinners, I was seated with my division's General Manager (GM). Once I learned he was also a Physics Major, we had plenty to talk about. A year later, I invited some Researchers to speak and demonstrate their 200 pel/inch display. I sent the GM a note saying he needed to see it. He arranged for a 7 AM meeting (after flying back from Asia). I

was comfortable saying he needed to see it and he knew me
well enough to fit the meeting into his schedule—which might
not have happened if we hadn't eaten together at the award
dinner.

Standards work is volunteer work, even though your
company pays your travel expenses. The number of hours
involved is more than any traditional work week. Being active
in the organization also means being willing to do extras. For
example, I like to write up the agreements. My colleague and I
co-edited the original JPEG standard. This work helped make
me IEEE Fellow, IBM Fellow, and eventually a member of the
National Academy of Engineering. Of course, I wasn't doing
it with any of these things in mind; we just needed a 'good in
hardware and good in software' standard our company would
use.

It would be impossible, and boring, to list all the people I've
met while giving back at work. Many of those people are
important, in terms of the power they wield within IBM or
within the scientific community. They have become a part of
my network. I know I can call on them. That doesn't mean
they will necessarily do what I ask them to do, but they will
listen to me. The GM shifted his schedule to be certain he saw
the demonstration of a new invention. The top technical
female in the company made a point of having lunch with a
new employee. Little things lead to great things. Your
network can help you along.

Promoting others

I heard a story once about two Annapolis graduates who
made a pact to support each other. Each went out of his way to
promote the other. They both made youngest-admirals the
same year. Later, I learned the Annapolis graduates were
actually Dutch Naval officers in the 16th century. In any case,
they both won when they used opportunities to help the other
advance.

Remember that PhD in my division whom I met at a TVC
meeting and then we invented together? After she left
Boulder, I visited her next location. I was asked if her resume
was true, and was pleased to be able to cite specific examples

from my own interaction to demonstrate its accuracy. After verifying her resume, the next question I received was, "Is she General Manager potential?" Last year she was the technical assistant to the top technical person in the company. Today she is running a laboratory in Russia—her dream. I find it deeply satisfying to look at her career and say, "I gave her a little boost in the right direction."

This is a woman who thought a vacation was writing only two papers instead of four. My main mentoring with her was to encourage her to take a real vacation. Once she did, she was hooked. Which leads us into …

The Importance of Vacations

No one is indispensable. I learned this the hard way when an auto accident knocked me out of commission for two days during high school. I was chair of a fund-raising dinner the next day and my friend had to take over from my notes. The dinner went off superbly. Not taking your vacation declares you are so unique and important that no one can share your load even temporarily.

Vacations serve four purposes, all of them equally important. You should take vacations because:

Your vacation benefits your team

You have a function within your team. When you are away on vacation, someone else is required to fulfill that function. For example, as a manager, I was usually the communicator, so the secretary directed requests for information to me. I quietly answered these time-consuming calls. When I was out of town for a week or more, the rest of the group dealt with the requests. It helped them gain visibility inside the company and they stopped taking for granted the work I did in this area. My workload didn't immediately rise to its previous level upon my return because others continued to deal with the work they took on in my absence. And I should note, they continued doing it quite well.

Even more importantly, my absence gave people room to grow and change their relationships (for the better) with other team members. People who barely talked to each other might be working on a joint project when I returned. As a manager, if I am gone for an extended period, someone else is appointed to cover for me. This vote of confidence helped them grow and, after attending a weekly management meeting, better understand what the job required.

Whatever your function, the person who handles it in your absence will grow, and they will learn to appreciate you. Both of these are worthy goals.

You should take vacations because:

Vacations allow you to recharge your internal batteries

My undergraduate university was only two hours from home. Usually, I got a ride with a friend, but I could take the bus if necessary. I went home for Thanksgiving, two weeks at Christmas, a week between winter and spring quarter, and usually at least one additional weekend per quarter. After finals, I needed to vegetate for several days before doing anything—including looking up high school friends.

When I went to graduate school at the University of Illinois, I was working my way through school. For the first time in my life, I was on a real budget. My second Christmas, I concluded I could not afford to fly home. Within a few weeks of this decision, my productivity dropped to zero and it stayed there until I looked into bus fares and decided I could afford the trip by bus. I never forgot the lesson.

As well as noticing a drop in productivity if I cancel a vacation, I notice my productivity is particularly high in anticipation of a vacation. I stop procrastinating over pesky tasks, because I don't want to face them on my return. Sometimes I work late before leaving to clear off my desk.

When I joined IBM, new hires with less than six months of employment in their first year did not qualify for vacation time. Since my start date was October, I only had Thanksgiving Day and Christmas Day as holidays. When I saw signs of my productivity dropping, I arranged to take a week of unpaid vacation and add some days of comp (compensatory) time at Christmas. This was 'just not done', but I believed the time with my family was essential to my well-being and ignored the signs of disapproval.

I would like to note, there is a difference between a one week vacation and a longer vacation. In my experience, it usually takes a week to unwind and truly relax. Then the real vacation can start.

Remember the PhD who learned to take vacations? She not only learned that vacations allow you to recharge, she also found a way to give back to the world community. She takes donated, used computer equipment to university friends in Eastern Europe. She researched the export laws and obtained the proper paperwork, so I know she doesn't cut corners. That donated computer equipment makes the difference between having a PhD program and not having one for the math department.

You should take vacations because:

It sets a good example for your children

I had a colleague whose idea of an extended vacation was to put a roof on his house. At one point, he had over one hundred and twenty-five weeks of accrued vacation. He planned for the accrued time to provide a tidy bonus at retirement time, but the rules changed and he had to take (or lose) 25% of his vacation each year. He lost most of it. I offered to plan a vacation for him but he wouldn't to pick a date until his teenaged daughters' summer plans had been established. Unfortunately, he never told them he was waiting on them.

To my horror, when he finally arranged a week off, his manager demanded he attend a crucial meeting scheduled (at the last minute) during his chosen week. I preached rebellion. He didn't listen.

Years later, I learned his father was a farmer. Cows don't take a vacation from making milk. His dad had never taken a vacation. Following his father's pattern, he was quite content to stay home and work. Several years later, when discussing the value of vacations with his daughters, I was glad to be able to share his story. Even if you don't think you want the hassle of a vacation, do it for your children to set a good example and give them stories to tell about their vacations.

As a child, my dad set a good example. He took us camping almost every weekend during the summer. We visited his parents for a week or two in June at least every other summer and often again for a week at Christmas. In June, our ultimate destination was Laguna Beach where we had a mini-reunion. His sister, some of his brothers, and their respective families joined us in an apartment complex overlooking the beach. It was common for some of his aunts and uncles with families to join in as well. Many of his relatives lived near Laguna Beach, so barbecues on the beach often had fifty to a hundred relatives enjoying the fruits of a deep sea fishing expedition. Since the meal was potluck, everyone contributed and it didn't matter how many people showed up. When you get to know your cousins and second-cousins as a child, you stay connected for the rest of your life even if you only meet every few years at reunions.

Dad always said he wanted to travel while he could still enjoy climbing cathedral steps and up into the towers for the view. The first time I heard that statement was as we were climbing Ulm (Germany) cathedral's five hundred-plus steps. I tell people, make sure you are retiring *to* something, not *from* something. The average life expectancy after retirement is shockingly low, particularly for those who have not developed an outside interest.

You should take vacations because:

You make priceless memories

Do you remember your first trip to Disneyland? Do you remember visiting your grandmother, or going fishing with your grandfather, or your first sight of the Grand Canyon? Those are the memories I'm talking about.

Vacations are a time to make memories—of people and of places—so that later in life you can take those memories out, and examine them and re-live the pleasure.

I don't have the desire or energy to do much planning in advance, so I find it wonderful when family members invite me to join them on vacation. For example, my youngest sister, her family, and some of her in-laws asked me to join them at a family camp. I thoroughly enjoyed doing things with my nieces and their cousins I would not have considered doing on my own. I know I never would have tried the rope-course without them.

Picture this. I wore a harness, so there was no way I could hurt myself, but I froze at the thought of crossing a log twenty feet above the ground. Halfway across, I fell. There I was, swinging in this harness with the ground at least a mile below me, and the log beside me. One of the instructors coached me and I got back onto the log and made my way across the abyss.

The zip-line came next. The zip-line stretched at least a block over an inlet in the lake. My first try I got about ten feet away from the dock and fell into the water. Fortunately, that was far enough to miss the shallow water. Since I had never been able to hold my weight with my arms, I was ready to quit, but the instructor noticed I had allowed my body to jerk against my hold rather than leaning out and smoothly transferring my weight. The next time, I held on until the middle of the lake where I let go and dropped into the water. A boat waited to pick me up. One more successful ride convinced me it wasn't a fluke. If you are the single relative invited along on a family vacation, you'll learn to do things you wouldn't otherwise consider.

Share your vacation with a friend. It's much more fun than going alone, and the experience will enrich your friendship. A friend of mine wanted to go to Hawaii. Both of her children were in college and unable to go off-season. She found a good deal on a package for us so we could visit four islands. We did a whirlwind tour. This was the first time I went snorkeling, and it was so much fun I've made it a part of my life now.

Looking back over the past decade, I am immensely grateful for the time I spent vacationing, particularly with family. The memories I made are precious to me. But most important are the times I spent with my mother. The extra time with Mom made it possible to deal with my loss when she passed. I am reminded of an adage, "No one ever lies on their death bed wishing they had spent more time working." Develop the habit of taking real vacations and treasuring your family now. You rarely know in advance when there won't be a tomorrow.

Summary

- Life is more than work
- Build a support network in the community
- Give back to your community
- Join and support a professional organization
- Take vacations

9

Interconnecting the Network

Company Fellow as Goal

*Wh*en I returned to Research after my two year leave of absence, my goal to become a company Fellow still headed my list. I've already told you how I went to each new manager. The conversation opened with these words, "The purpose of this appointment is to be sure you understand my goal is to become a company Fellow. Any ideas or suggestions on how I can get there?" My opening was always followed by a fruitful half-hour dialog. Your managers and mentors cannot help you accomplish your goals if they don't know what your goals are.

Writing the JPEG book was one step towards accomplishing my goal. Every Fellow I knew at Research had written a classic reference book in their field. I moved into Marketing for almost three years because I knew staying exclusively in Research would limit my breadth of experience and make it harder to become a Fellow. Working for Burlington also fit into this scheme. The more divisions supporting your appointment, the more likely you are to be appointed. The better known you are within your company, the more likely you are to advance.

My road to Fellow wasn't strewn with rose petals. At one point, I thought I had been told to look for work outside the company. When I took my leave of absence, I didn't know if I'd ever have a job to come back to. But perseverance paid off.

Over the years, I learned a lot about myself. I work better and am more productive when I work with other people. Maybe this is true of you as well. Or maybe you work better when people leave you alone and let you have your head. Only you can answer that question about yourself, but if you want to progress in your career, you need to consider the question and find your answer.

I've stressed the importance of networking, and I'm going to stress it again. No one gets to where they want to be without help from those around them. You need to make contacts, both within your company and on the outside. You need to keep those contacts fresh. Don't ignore the people who help you. To do so gives them the impression that you only wanted what you could get from them—that you didn't value them for themselves.

The second time I was asked to transfer to Boulder full time was a few years ago. This time I was willing to consider it. I didn't realize the manager who invited me was more interested in my membership in the Academy than he was in my technical skills. He had recently learned the only Academy of Technology member in the Printing Systems Division was retiring. The retiree had been the manager's primary sponsor for nomination to the Academy.

I successfully sponsored the manager to the Academy a year later. I thought he would be president of the Academy within a few years, but he didn't attend his first annual meeting. He accepted an offer from another company and left IBM the same week. When I heard about it through the grapevine, at first I didn't believe it. I strongly recommend that if you change jobs, you notify your mentors and the people who have sponsored you as soon the news becomes public rather than let them learn about your departure from others. Those people may be important to you later in life, and you don't want them to feel you used and abused them.

Becoming an IEEE Fellow

Several years ago, I received a call from an ex-IEEE President in my company asking if I was an IEEE Senior Member because he wanted to nominate me for IEEE Fellow, and being a Senior Member was a prerequisite. I thought you became an IEEE Senior Member because someone else nominated you. Over the previous ten years, I had noticed no one thought I was good enough to nominate, but I never asked anyone nor planted any seeds. You can imagine my embarrassment when the caller said, "You can nominate yourself. I'll send you the paperwork. Have three IEEE Senior Members or Fellows act as references."

I contacted three friends, and all three were willing to be references. In my move from New York to Vermont, I lost the paperwork and I forgot about the nomination until I received a letter from IEEE. They had three impressive references for IEEE Senior Member on file, but unless I filled out the self-nomination form and returned it within a month, the references would expire. A blank form was enclosed. Within a day, I returned the completed form. A few months later, I received a congratulatory letter.

I believed being an external Fellow would make it easier to become an internal Fellow, so a few months after I returned from my unpaid leave, I started the process to become an IEEE Fellow. Unfortunately, it was only a few weeks before the deadline to submit and my references didn't have time to respond. I wrote a reminder in my Day-timer to do it again nine months later.

The following December, I contacted the ex-IEEE President who had wanted to nominate me. He was still willing, and asked me to work with another person to complete the form. The process was slow and painful until I asked to see four successful nominations. Then it became fun because I could interpret the questions according to the answers in the successful nominations. I also saw how to shrink words because the answers had a maximum character count. I recommend asking for copies of successfully completed nominations any time you need to complete one of these complex forms.

When I coach people through the process today, I encourage them to use the process as a time to evaluate their professional life. Questions like, "What do you want to be known for in 100 years?" help decide the area and the twenty words that will define your impact. You need to know the general characteristics and goals of the group who will evaluate your nomination before filling out forms because your application should focus on things important to that organization. Once you have taken some time to answer the questions thoughtfully, you pick out your fifteen most important contributions to support your application. You are asked for your professional activities. At first I thought I had nothing to place in that section until I realized my favorite conference was cosponsored by an IEEE society.

My coordinator approached my suggested references to confirm they were willing to write references. When I nominate someone, I usually do the same. I want to know they will write the letter. With IEEE, about half of the eight allowed references should be from outside your company. If fewer than five references respond, the nomination is not considered. As coordinator, follow-up is part of the process. If you think enough of a person to nominate them for something, finish the job properly.

I listed the facsimile data compression standard and the JPEG standard as some of my contributions. At the time of their creation, only my company believed the standards should be in software as well as hardware.

Once the paperwork is submitted, you wait eight months. I remembered I would hear in November, but forgot notification would be on the 15th. On November 2nd, I concluded I hadn't made it. My reaction was, "I gave it my best effort. I don't know how to do it better. I don't think I'll try again." On November 15th, I received a congratulatory e-mail. What a surprise!

A decade later I learned the probability of making IEEE Fellow on the first try is slim. In some cases, the odds can be less than one in ten. However, the odds improve radically on the second try and are closer to one in three. It's like being introduced to your neighbor. Once you've met someone, suddenly you see him everywhere. The review committee has a back-log of people they looked at the previous year, and have been noticing ever since. Even if your nomination is rejected, during the next year they notice your name all over the place and are prepared to agree on the second try.

Keep a copy of your nomination form. My IEEE nomination has been used to nominate me for other awards. Around 1999, my second-line management called for a copy of my resume. He asked if I had any other list of accomplishments. I assume the information I provided was used to nominate me for IBM Fellow. Some years later, a friend asked me for my long resume and any other useful information. He nominated me successfully for the National Academy of Engineering. The extra effort can be well worth it.

Be a nominator—it's called networking. Most professional societies have awards to recognize excellence within the profession. Ask for and use copies of past successful nomination forms when completing your paperwork. This makes the process easier for the nominator and increases the chances of success. Nominating someone for a professional award is a lot of work, but a successful result makes the work worthwhile.

Academy of Technology

A few months after I returned from my leave of absence, I received a call from a complete stranger inside IBM asking if I wanted to be nominated for the IBM Academy of Technology. He explained that a few of them tried to nominate on merit and they had selected me. In the early 90's I'd been on two data compression task forces for the Academy, but I assumed it was nothing more than an umbrella organization for publishing reports. I asked some questions, and then I tracked down some other members and asked them questions. The Academy, a self-electing body of about three hundred technical experts, was created while I was in Marketing.

Participating in Academy work (giving back at work) is a strong prerequisite for being elected to the Academy. Three current members must support your nomination and write endorsements. Your life work is condensed to about one page. If you have ever read seventy to one hundred highly qualified candidates' credentials, you can understand voting is hard work. Fortunately, you have thirty votes.

I was elected to the Academy during my first year back at Research. When I attended my first annual meeting, I was surprised to meet old friends and colleagues from all over the world. They had disappeared from my radar screen when I went into Marketing. I assumed they left the company when I didn't hear from them after I returned. It didn't occur to me they had switched fields in order to find safer harbors. If I'd kept in contact with my network, I wouldn't have been so surprised.

When I joined IBM, I intended to create a network of 'doers'. In Research, I was encouraged to talk to developers in all divisions. Some of the divisions had more restrictions—primarily time. Much of my value to IBM lay in my ability to provide introductions to developers who needed to connect with each other. I hoped over time some of these doers would work their way up in the company and still be willing to look to me for advice. I like being listened to. Election to the Academy renewed my faith in that strategy. When I got to Boulder, I discovered one of my friends refers to Academy members as baby fellows. All new Fellows, if not already members, are admitted automatically.

In Research, if I talked to a colleague for an hour, I was taking an hour out of his or her personal life, but I needed more people to work with. My Research management allowed me to transfer to Boulder for a year or two. They wanted to be sure the transfer would work out, so they suggested I visit Boulder in October and November for two weeks at a time. If things didn't work out, it wouldn't be too late to back out.

My transfer to Boulder was critical to my appointment as Fellow. It began as a temporary assignment. In Boulder, I blossomed. There were real problems needing real solutions, and hundreds of people to interact with. I worked with eight different groups of people and saw a need for my skills. Amazingly, I could even help the hardware design people. I had requested some experiments to help define the properties of a new printer. I borrowed a 30x hand-held illuminated microscope from the software engineer—a trade show favor. When I examined the print samples, my description of the quality was, "Garbage." Eventually I realized everyone else was using 5x and 10x passive loops. When they borrowed my borrowed microscope, they agreed with my evaluation.

The microscope was printed with the name and number of the company who had provided it as a trade-show favor. After a few false starts and misunderstandings, I ordered a large quantity of them. They arrived in Boulder and I passed them out, considering the investment a major contribution to future image quality.

In 1998, before my temporary assignment to Boulder, I had already seen an increase in my invention disclosure activity. That year five patents were filed and six new disclosures were submitted. The first year in Boulder, I submitted ten more invention disclosures. These latest inventions were with developers. In most cases, I handled the details because I didn't have product code deadlines. One more patent was filed. My second year in Boulder, twenty-three patent applications were filed and another sixteen invention disclosures submitted. When you compare this with about thirty-six patents filed in the previous twenty-five years, you can see the invention productivity increase. The magic, in my opinion, was being close to real problems. Solutions that go quickly into products have to be filed quickly too.

Giving up hope

Since I was on temporary assignment, my Research manager gave me my 1999 yearly evaluation on one of my periodic trips back to the Research Center. After a phenomenal year, my evaluation seemed mediocre. I believed I needed a top evaluation in order to become an IBM Fellow. That night in the hotel room, I bawled for hours because I felt I had to give up my goal. At the end of the evening, I was at peace again. I wasn't going to quit trying to act like a Fellow even if I never became one.

The next day, I sat down for lunch with the female head of HR at Research. Her first words were, "Joan, how are we going to make you a Fellow." I answered, "It is my goal, but it's impossible. I can't seem to get a superior evaluation and I'm not a Master Inventor." She looked me straight in the eye and said, "You are on the short list." I'd never heard of the short list. "What short list?" So she told me, "The list of nominated candidates in the CEO's office."

That night I made out my Fellow's agenda—the list of problems I wanted to work on as a company Fellow. At the top of my list was to adopt a college in Kentucky and try to get some of its students placed with the company.

When I looked over the list, I thought, "There is nothing about this list that says I have to be a Fellow to do them. I am going to get started and not wait." As I've said before, at IBM people get promotions after they are doing the job. I wanted to act like a Fellow. I also wanted to grow in the direction of doing big, important things.

Once I knew management held a higher opinion of me than I had previously assumed, I felt able to 'take power' and move to a different level of action. Expectations and perceptions make a huge difference in how we see ourselves. I needed to know others thought I could be a Fellow, in order to feel free to act like a Fellow.

On the same trip, I discovered the first female Fellow had been appointed my official mentor a year earlier. Wish I'd known then. It didn't take long to track her down and start asking questions. I explained that no one told me about the appointment and asked, "Did anyone ask you?" She remembered agreeing to do it, but when I never called, she didn't think anything more about it. Knowing I had a real chance of reaching my goal, I had questions—including what happens after you become a Fellow? She didn't sugar-coat her answer. Nothing changes unless you change it. I found this all the more reason to start making changes now.

Several years previously, a person I had hired into the company became a Fellow. When I asked him how much advance warning he had, he said three months. I took his words literally and when I hadn't heard by mid-March, I assumed there was no hope for 2001. I mentioned this to an executive in the division. She called back in a few hours to say the decision had not been made.

In the process, she learned I planned to leave Boulder at the end of my third year. I shared with her my Fellow's agenda. She suggested she could create the kind of job I desired in Boulder, so we reached an agreement. At the end of the year, I would transfer under her and start on my Fellow's agenda. I'd pretend I was a Fellow and get going.

One Monday morning in late March, I got a call from the assistant to the Director of the Research Lab wanting to arrange a fifteen-minute call with me. "Are you available right now?" I was. The Director came on and congratulated me because I'd been appointed Fellow. The public announcement would be at the Corporate Technical Recognition Event (CTRE) in Florida at the end of May.

I went alone to my first CTRE, but after meeting people with their siblings, parents, adult children, and good friends, I saw the light. Since then, I invite family members to accompany me. It's much more fun to share the event with someone you love.

The company CEO announced the seven new Fellows at the first morning meeting. Afterwards, the Fellows and their guests were invited to meet with him. Since he made the final selection, my impression that he actually knows who I am is probably correct.

The night after the new Fellows were announced, I decided to start the Master Inventor program for my division and to qualify for it here in Boulder. My efforts to learn how to start the program brought the issue to the attention of my manager. He decided to sponsor the program, but he wanted it to be secret until the program was ready to launch. I almost blew it when I sent him a note saying I had formed a team of top inventors to define a mission statement. My team became a subset of the complete group.

As a Research Staff Member, I never considered publicity important; however, it was a part of my new job. Shortly after I became a Fellow, the local papers interviewed me. One of the photographers remembered his JPEG pictures of the Broncos (Super Bowl) making the evening papers in New York. Now his camera has a wireless modem. A few minutes after he takes a picture, he can discuss it with his editor on the phone. It's a wonderful feeling to know you have made a difference in the world.

A Fellow's Agenda

What comes after Fellow?

At the Printing Systems Division recognition event on
Maui, the keynote speaker was Lou Holtz, the ex-Notre Dame
football coach. He shared his experience of growing bored
maintaining Super Bowl status. It's why he left football.
Several years later, he returned to his alma mater and helped
them win a bowl game two years later. He insisted it is
important to keep growing. This made me start thinking about
what follows achieving Fellow.

As I said in the beginning, being a Fellow means freedom to
me. I have the freedom to choose projects that will impact the
world. I have the freedom to help others do the same. And
one of the things I learned along the way is I have always had
the freedom to choose what I think about what happens around
me. You have it too, so embrace it and move forward. Change
your world.

One of the early items on my "Fellow's Agenda" was to
grow a mature business. In potentially declining markets, it is
hard to grow a business without some out-of-box thinking,
which happens to be my specialty. For several years, I saw no
effect from the seeds of thought I planted. Then suddenly
everyone seemed to assume growth was the direction we
should take. The debate became "when should we" rather than
"should we?" The details are not for public consumption, but
unless the group is asking the question and publicly discussing,
"How can we/should we grow?" how can they expect to grow?

As a Fellow, I focus on growing the next generation of
leaders. Instead of talking about how to succeed, I have mini-
projects with others so they can follow their passion and
achieve success. They leverage my contacts to find outlets
beyond Boulder. Making the other person drive the project
frees me up to have fifteen to twenty projects. You may not
have the same freedom to choose your projects, but you have
the freedom to share your knowledge. You have the freedom
to contribute to the growth of your company and the growth of
your colleagues.

Letters of recommendation are easy to write when you have worked with someone and believe in their capabilities. There is a certain ring of authenticity when you are able to say honestly, "John Doe is creative and at the same time practical. We submitted four invention disclosures on our joint work last year and they were all filed. John Doe has interacted with the rest of the company to transfer these inventions into products." As a Fellow, I get to write lots of letters of recommendation. Your letters of recommendation may not carry the same weight as mine, but they carry weight. Look for opportunities to recommend your colleagues.

Moving others up the value chain was discussed in earlier chapters. It has been a part of my Fellow's Agenda since before I became a Fellow. Recently someone compared my mini-projects to being a thesis advisor. I found the comparison intriguing because I am the co-advisor for one of my mentees. After about a year and a half of research and filing patent applications, we realized her project would make a great PhD thesis. I've already related the story of how another mentor of hers joined me to invite her favorite teacher from her Master's work to lunch. At the end of the meal, my friend and I knew she had found her advisor. She sees her official advisor about once a month and we usually talk daily when both of us are in town.

She hopes to finish her degree in another year, just three years from official admission into the program. She did all this while raising three sons with the help of a supportive husband and working full time, but she could not have accomplished it without a little bit of effort on the part of her mentors and a lot of effort on her part.

I started a mini-project with an engineer who was already in the PhD program. It had never occurred to him to ask the question, "Who needs to use this *now* before it's finished and all wrapped up." Some people are what I call 'scientists,' enthralled by the elegance of a solution. Others I call 'engineers.' Their first reaction is, "Who will use it, and what will it cost." Our mini-project was to connect the engineer (network) with the rest of the company. Once he realized he didn't have to do it alone, he did most of the connecting. His thesis advisor was already working with other people from the company. They had noticed his work, just didn't know he was also in the company. He has made the transition to 'scientist'.

Several of my mini-projects involve helping another person learn to get through the company invention disclosure process. It can be daunting until you have done it once. I have a good friend whom I consider company Fellow caliber. He has outside visibility, published papers, strong impact on the company, and is well known inside the company. But he had no company inventions. I suggested we team up to get him over the hurdle of the patenting process. Our first invention related to protecting Heating, Ventilation, and Air Conditioning (HVAC) systems from terrorist attacks. After our first patent application was filed, he commented, "This is just problem solving. I do that all the time." He has learned to ask the questions, "Is it novel?" and "Will the solution have business value to another company?"

One of the goals I wrote down soon after I became a Fellow was to be able to look back on my career and point to ten Fellows I had helped along their way. So far I can only point to two, but there's still time.

As a Fellow, I give group mentoring talks, as well as doing one on one mentoring. I've seen from the talks that people are hungry for frank information about the workplace. I sincerely hope this book will help to clue employees in to the requirements of the workplace.

Summary

- Encourage your mentees to leverage your network
- Share your goals and ask for advice on achieving them
- With freedom comes responsibility; grow the next generation
- Think big

*H*aving come to the end of this book, I am amazed that the first draft was written by spending an hour or two most mornings writing stories to my father. I began the day after Thanksgiving, and slowed down sometime in May with my 106th e-mail. The stories came from memory, so as I said in the preface, they shouldn't be taken literally. It doesn't matter whether the words, or even the facts, are correct. What matters is the lessons I drew from the memory (accurate or not). Hopefully, my experiences have been relevant to you. You will make mistakes, and you will go through a process of trial and error. Maybe my experiences will allow you to avoid the same mistakes and help you along in your career without the same trials and errors. Many of my stories came to mind because I use them frequently in mentoring sessions. This book is intended to act in part as your mentor on The Basics (Part I), then The Next Steps (Part II), and finally Pulling it all Together (Part III).

I have always had the freedom to make choices, and so do you. Don't confuse power with freedom. As a Fellow, I have the power to make choices and not suffer certain adverse consequences. If I make unwise choices, I still have to face the consequences. You have the freedom to choose the work you do, and to choose to be unemployed if the work offered to you is not acceptable. You have the freedom to choose to help others and to seek out help from others. You have the freedom to join your professional society and to become known within your field. You have the freedom to choose how you react to what happens around you. Embrace your freedom and make wise choices. Take charge of your career and change the world.

I still have a large bookcase covered with several inches of clippings, books, and presentations for each of the original twenty chapters I intended to have. The de-cluttering and organizing I did prior to writing was not wasted effort. The process reminded me of stories and helped me to organize my thoughts. As I contemplate the treasure trove of mentoring ideas partly hidden by the door, I wonder if there will be another book. My co-author suggested it when we realized how much we would have to cut from the original e-mails. Of course, her idea of heaven is writing seven days a week. I insisted it would be at least another decade before I would be ready to tackle another book. However, I have resumed my e-mails to Dad.

If this book has helped you, please share it. There is no greater gift you can give a teacher than to take what you learned and carry it on.

$\mathcal{D}$r. **Joan L. Mitchell** lives in Longmont, CO and works in Boulder. She graduated from Stanford University with a B.S. in physics in 1969 and received her M.S. and PhD. degrees in physics from the University of Illinois at Champaign-Urbana in 1971 and 1974 respectively. She immediately joined the IBM T. J. Watson Research Center in New York in an Exploratory Printing Technologies Group. She participated in the CCITT Study Group VIII facsimile committee in 1978 and 1979. She was a first line manager (in addition to research responsibilities) for a total of 11 years. She was in ImagePlus Marketing for almost three years from 1989 to 1991. She was on the JPEG international standards committee from 1987 to 1994 and became co-editor of the first JPEG standard. She co-authored a book on JPEG. In 1994, she took a two year leave of absence. During that time, she co-authored a book on MPEG and taught a semester at the University of Illinois.

Since 1999, Dr. Mitchell has worked in Boulder, CO with the IBM Printing Systems Division. She is co-inventor on more than 70 patents including a personal patent on a new scuba wet suit. She was elected to the IBM Academy of Technology in 1997 and became an IEEE Fellow in 1999. In 2001, Dr. Joan L. Mitchell became the 168th IBM Fellow appointed (and the seventh female). Fellow is IBM's highest technical rank as well as being an executive position. In 2004, Dr. Mitchell was elected a member of the National Academy of Engineering. She is a member of APS, IEEE, IS&T, and Sigma Xi.

Dr. Mitchell chose mentoring and growing the next generation to be a significant portion of her Fellow's agenda. This book shares with a wider audience some of the lessons she learned along the way to IBM Fellow.

Nancy Walker Mitchell lives in Henderson, Nevada where she writes full time. She is married, with two grown sons and four grandchildren. She has written technical manuals as works for hire, and her first published book, *Surviving Your Student Loans* came about as a result of working in the student loan collections industry. The book describes various types of federally guaranteed student loans and the techniques for managing them effectively. She describes it as her gift to struggling students. Nancy primarily writes mysteries and is working on a series of cozies based in Las Vegas. Since her protagonist is a stripper, Nancy has enjoyed doing the research required to keep her series technically accurate. "You gotta do Your Research", the short story she wrote after one of her ventures to the strip clubs, appears in *Writers Bloc*. Other works in progress include the memoirs of a woman who taught on the Havasupai Reservation from 1949 through 1951, a series of young adult science fiction (co-authored with Joan L. Mitchell), and numerous other works of fiction.

Acknowledgements

$\mathcal{M}$any people have made a difference in my life. I can only name a few here and give special thanks to a supportive extended family. Thanks to the late Prof. Mary Sunseri for teaching me that being female is special; to Prof. David Lazarus for being a superb teacher and the best possible thesis advisor; to Dr. Keith S. Pennington for hiring me and for daily lunches with the new employee; to Dr. William B. Pennebaker for leading by example; to Peter Capek for giving me access to a display terminal and teaching me to "beg forgiveness instead of asking permission"; to Karen Anderson Magerlein for hard work on joint inventions and insisting I read Tom DeMarco's book; to James M. Morgan for being willing to test for bugs after midnight in our JPEG proposal code; to Dave Liddell for coaching me at midnight via telephone when I was at JPEG meetings in Europe; to Dr. Fred Mintzer for believing in me and allowing me to take the leave of absence and then giving me a job to return to; to Dr. Paul Horn for helping to make me a Fellow; to Dr. Nick Donofrio for including me in the thousands he mentors and helping to make me a Fellow; to Jeffrey Paterra for believing an IBM Fellow's job is to do exactly what he/she wants to do; to my assistant Katheryne Raile for keeping me organized; to my ATSM Jan Reed for not letting things fall through the cracks; to Dr. Nenad Rejavec for convincing me to move to Colorado; to Arianne Hinds for always wanting to know "why"; to Yue Qiao for teaching me as much as I teach her; to David Ward for asking for mentoring from a PhD; to Jay Smith for proving it works to find your thesis advisor before applying to graduate school; to Jim Treinin for those mentoring luncheons every six months; to Barbara McLane for making appointments to mentor me; to Dr. Sharon Nunes for being my current official mentor; to Dr. Sandra K. Johnson for mentoring me more than I do her during our mentoring sessions; to Dr. Paul McKenney for being enthusiastic about the book; and to Karen Gilleland for showing us how to tighten the book. To all of you who mentored me, to all of you who listened when I mentored and particularly to all of you who asked for this book, thank you.

My acknowledgements would not be complete without thanking the many people who helped me find a title. —Joan L. Mitchell

*M*any people have had a profound effect on my life as well. Don Mitchell, my husband, stands behind me in my efforts to turn writing into a career instead of a hobby. Ruth Proud Sheehy spent hours teaching me the craft of writing and continues to do so via e-mail. My extended family, in-laws and outlaws and all of those born to the clan, have taken the time to read everything I send to them, even when they have no interest in the subject matter. Special thanks to my parents, Dell and Inez Walker, and Jean Hodges who keep encouraging me to write—and then to do something with my books. The Henderson Writer's Group also deserves special thanks for their assistance in mastering the craft and their encouragement to get the work out there. Of course, no thank you could be complete without mentioning Joan L. Mitchell, who gave me the opportunity to co-author this book. She could have managed with an editor, and she knew me well enough to know I wouldn't be able to stick to strictly editing. But she trusted me with her words anyway. —Nancy Walker Mitchell

Bibliography

Don Aslett, *Clutter's Last Stand: It's Time to De-Junk Your Life!*, 2nd ed., Adams Media: Avon, MA © 2005.

Debra A. Benton, *How to Think Like a CEO: The 22 Vital Traits You Need to Be the Person at the Top*, Warner Books: New York © 1999.

Debra A. Benton, *Lions Don't Need to Roar: Using the Leadership Power of Professional Presence to Stand Out, Fit In and Move Ahead*, Warner Books: New York © 1993.

Edwin C. Bliss, *Doing it Now*, Bantam Books: New York © 1984.

Edwin C. Bliss, *Getting Things Done: The ABCs of Time Management*, Bantam Books: New York © 1976.

Robert M. Bramson, *Coping with Difficult People: The Proven-Effective Battle Plan That Has Helped Millions Deal with the Troublemakers in Their Lives at Home and at Work*, Dell Publishing: New York © 1981.

Jeff Campbell and The Clean Team, *Speed Cleaning*, 2nd ed., Dell Publishing: New York © 1991.

Donald K. Clifford and Richard E. Cavanagh, *The Winning Performance: How America's High Growth Midsize Companies Succeed*, Bantam: New York ©1985.

Jim Collins, *Good to Great: Why Some Companies Make the Leap ... and Others Don't*, Harper Business: New York © 2001.

Stephen R. Covey, *The 7 Habits of Highly Effective People: Restoring the Character Ethic*, Simon and Schuster: New York ©1989.

Stephanie Culp, How to Get Organized When You Don't Have the Time, Writers Digest Books: Cincinnati, OH © 1986.

Tom DeMarco and Timothy Lister, *Peopleware: Productive Projects and Teams*, Dorset House: New York © 1987.

Suzette Haden Elgin, *The Gentle Art of Verbal Self-Defense*, Prentice-Hall: Englewood Cliffs, NJ, © 1980.

Louis V. Gerstner Jr., Who Says Elephant's Can't Dance?, Harper Business: New York © 2002.

Betty Lehan Harragan, *Games Your Mother Never Taught You: Corporate Gamesmanship for Women*, Warner Books: New York © 1977.

Pat Heim with Susan K. Golant, *Hardball for Women: Winning at the Game of Business*, Lowell House: Los Angeles © 1992.

Robert Heinlein, *Citizen of the Galaxy*, Ace Books: New York © 1957.

Robert Heinlein, *Double Star*, Signet: New York © 1956.

Paul Hersey and Kenneth H. Blanchard, *Management of Organizational Behavior: Utilizing Human Resource*, Prentice-Hall: Englewood Cliffs, NJ © 1972.

Alan Lakein, *How to Get Control of Your Time & Your Life*, P. H. Wyden: New York © 1973.

David Lazarus and Manfred Raether, *Practical Physics: How Things Work*, Stipes Publishing Company: Champaign, IL 1979.

Bibliography

Michael LeBoeuf, *GMP: The Greatest Management Principle in the World*, Putnam: New York © 1985.

Harvey Mackay, *Sharkproof: Get the Job You Want, Keep the Job You Love... in Today's Frenzied Job Market*, Harper Business: New York © 1993.

Catherine Marshall, *Something More*, McGraw-Hill: New York © 1974.

Robert L. Montgomery, *Memory Made Easy*, Learn Incorporated: Laurel, NJ © 1984.

George Polya, *How to Solve It: A New Aspect of Mathematical Method*, 2nd ed., Princeton University Press: Princeton, NJ © 1957.

Kevin G. Rivette and David Kline, *Rembrandts in the Attic: Unlocking the Hidden Value of Patents,* Harvard Business School Press: Boston, MA © 2000.

Pam Young and Peggy Jones, *The Side-Tracked Home Executives: From Pigpen to Paradise*, Warner Books: New York ©1981.

Index

This book produced at the
IBM Boulder Infoprint Center
Boulder • Colorado
U.S.A.

For more information about fulfilling your printing needs,
please contact one of our customer service representatives:

Diana Wingerberg
phone: (303) 924-6678
email: dwing@us.ibm.com

Anthony Sarno
phone: (303) 924-6561
email: asarno@us.ibm.com